ADAMS

SERVICE, SERVICE, SERVICE

D1056845

Business titles from Adams Media Corporation

Accounting for the New Business, by Christopher R. Malburg
Adams Businesses You Can Start Almanac
Adams Streetwise Consulting, by David Kintler
Adams Streetwise Customer-Focused Selling, by Nancy Stephens
Adams Streetwise Do-It-Yourself Advertising, by Sarah White and John Woods
Adams Streetwise Hiring Top Performers, by Bob Adams and Peter Veruki
Adams Streetwise Managing People, by Bob Adams, et al.
Adams Streetwise Small Business Start-Up, by Bob Adams
All-in-One Business Planner, by Christopher R. Malburg
Buying Your Own Business, by Russell Robb
Entrepreneurial Growth Strategies, by Lawrence W. Tuller
Exporting, Importing, and Beyond, by Lawrence W. Tuller
How to Become Successfully Self-Employed, by Brian R. Smith
How to Start and Operate a Successful Business, by David E. Rye
Management Basics, by John & Shirley Payne
Managing People, by Darien McWhirter
Marketing Magic, by Don Debelak
The Personnel Policy Handbook for Growing Companies, by Darien McWhirter
Selling 101: A Course for Business Owners and Non-Sales People,
by Michael T. McGaulley
Service, Service, Service: A Secret Weapon for Your Growing Business,
by Steve Albrecht
The Small Business Legal Kit, by J. W. Dicks
The Small Business Valuation Book, by Lawrence W. Tuller

ADAMS

SERVICE, SERVICE, SERVICE

A Secret Weapon for Your Growing Business

STEVE ALBRECHT

Adams Media Corporation
Holbrook, Massachusetts

Published by Adams Media Corporation
260 Center Street, Holbrook, MA 02343

ISBN: 1-55850-758-2

Printed in the United States of America.

J I H G F E D C

Library of Congress Cataloging-in-Publication Data
Albrecht, Steve.
Service, service, service : a secret weapon for your growing business / Steve Albrecht.
p.   cm.
Includes bibliographical references and index.
ISBN 1-55850-758-2 (pb.)
1. Customer service. I. Title. II. Series.
HF5415.5.A435   1994
658.8'12—dc20   94-32649
CIP

This publication is designed to provide accurate and authoritative information with regard to the subject matter covered. It is sold with the understanding that the publisher is not engaged in rendering legal, accounting, or other professional advice. If legal advice or other expert assistance is required, the services of a competent professional person should be sought.
— From a *Declaration of Principles* jointly adopted by a Committee of the American Bar Association and a Committee of Publishers and Associations

This book is available at quantity discounts for bulk purchases.
For information, call 1-800-872-5627 (in Massachusetts, 781-767-8100).

Visit our home page at http://www.adamsmedia.com

"To my creditors, whose increasing impatience
has made this book necessary."

—JAMES RONALD
upon the publication of his 1940 book, *This Way Out*.

_____

And to Carly,
who demands, and gets,
the best service Leslie and I can give.

Table of Contents

Foreword

by Karl Albrecht

It's been said that the greatest obstacle to learning something is believing you already know it. Too many of the people trying to lead businesses today are handicapped by their own belief systems. They believe they know what customers want. They believe they know what creates a true, sustainable competitive advantage. They believe they know what the people in their organizations are capable of contributing, what they're thinking, and what they want out of their work lives. Much of what most of them believe is wrong.

It's time for senior managers to un-learn much of what they've learned, or believe they've learned. And more importantly, it's time for *organizations* to un-learn and re-learn if they are going to survive and thrive in this new and chaotic business environment.

That learning process is at the heart of the message presented by this book. A true customer focus, a true service focus, requires a fairly fundamental re-learning process that goes to the deepest levels of the organizational culture. It requires an open and honest effort to discern the truth of customer value and an aggressive determination to implement it in a very thorough way.

All of us in the business world still have much to learn if we are to move our organizations beyond the level of slogans and platitudes about customer service. Nearly 10 years after the publication of *Service America!*, which launched the so-called service revolution in the USA and eventually abroad, can we really say most of our businesses are truly customer-focused? Just consult your own recent experience and you'll see that most of the real opportunities still lie before us.

With this book, Steve Albrecht tells us it's time to get serious about it. It's time for those in charge of businesses to engage the practical issues and challenges of moving their organizations into the new age of customer focus.

Such a book couldn't have come at a better time. The world-wide movement toward downsizing, delayering, deconstruction, and shaking up of organizations favors a new breed of business and a new breed of business leader. In the future, the game will be won not by the megafirms that merely rely on size and accumulated capital to create competitive advantage, but by the more focused, flexible, and customer-committed enterpises.

Those leaders who can discern the real truth of business success for their enterprises and implement that truth in their everyday operations have the best chance of winning in the increasingly global business battle. Steve Albrecht has provided a battle plan that can have great value for those who will make use of it.

Bio Note: Karl Albrecht is one of the most widely-quoted authors and consultants on the subject of service management in the world. His bestselling business books include the landmark *Service America!*, *At America's Service*, and *The Only Thing That Matters*. His most recent book, *The Northbound Train*, was published by AMACOM.

Preface

No matter what you sell—products or services or a combination of both—the problems you face as a small-businessperson are still the same: How do I create, market and sell our products or services to the best of my ability? How do I hire, train, and keep the best employees to help us reach this goal? What is the best way to organize my company so that things run smoothly? How do I manage the money, the costs, the inventory, and the physical and psychological assets that make up our company?

Amidst all of these questions comes several important ones: How do I attract, serve, and keep customers? What do the concepts relating to "service quality" and "customer value" really mean to me and my firm?

Few business topics have generated as much need for organizational tinkering as the concept of service management. Not content with the fact that all customers want to be served well, treated fairly, and shown decency, courtesy, and respect, many business book and article writers have set about dissecting and analyzing this not-so-new idea to the nth degree.

This book seeks to reinforce one crystalline message:

> Business is what if you don't have, you'll go out of. The only way to survive in our ever-changing service economy is to get customers and keep them. You can offer the best products or services in the world, but if no one comes to you to buy them, you will fail. Business success—your business success—starts and ends with the type of service to your customers that meets their needs and even exceeds their expectations.

As obvious as this may appear, sometimes its clarity is lost on its audience. Instead of looking just over the steering wheel as they drive the company car down the new economic superhighway, too many business owners, operators, executives, and managers attempt to look three off-ramps down the road. If you can't focus on what's right in front of you, you'll crash. And so it goes with the small-businessperson as well.

The size of your company or your balance sheet is a relative thing. In some respects, big businesses and small businesses are as similar as they are different. They both sell products and services, win or lose money, and succeed or fail the same way—one customer at a time. But this book will suggest that perhaps the small business has several unique advantages over the big guys in terms of having more inherent flexibility, less bureaucratic management, and fewer things to interfere with the way the front-line service employees reach the customer.

And if it's true that in business nothing happens until someone sells something to somebody, it's even more true that no business can survive unless it directs all its efforts toward serving the people who ultimately do the buying—the customers.

Unless the strategies, systems, and the service employees are all centered around the needs and expectations of the customer, the business will not thrive.

From its initial beginning in the early 1980s to now, the leaders of our service revolution have tried to preach one message: "Change your company so that it focuses on the needs and expectations of the customer. And do it right now."

Service, Service, Service offers the direction, the leadership, and the marching plan for any small business organization's entry into the service revolution. Whether you've been engaged in the operation of a small business one year or one dozen years, this book preaches the same simple message that started the service revolution: It's the customer.

This book covers a subject—the management of service and the way to turn your organization into a customer-focused entity—

that is timely, current, and filled with examples that make it real for today's small-business owner. Since most small-business owners are short on time and long on work, this book will get right to the point: orient your company around the customer and do it in an organized, methodical fashion.

The book skips the trivial platitudes, the faulty ideas for new versions of the same old employee "smile training" classes, and the bane of all service quality programs—reckless enthusiasm not backed by significant change or top-management commitment. It tells small-businesspeople what they must do to succeed in the ongoing, ever-changing service economy that is now a global reality.

Economists, government statistical forecasters, and industry analysts can talk about production and output and the number of widgets produced per machine, per employee, per factory, per day. Everything in business *still* starts and ends with the customer.

This book is aimed at you if you're a small-business owner, operator, executive, franchisee, manager, or supervisor who has questions about how to make your company more service-driven and more customer-focused. By concentrating on direct actions, step-by-step approaches, and simple models, rather than hard-to-use theories or business school textbook-philosophies, this book will empower you so that you may empower the people who work with and for you.

And whether you're new to the subject or more familiar with it, the book will emphasize specific actions, duties, and operational strategies that can serve as a road map for your company to follow, regardless of where it is along the service management time line.

To play devil's advocate for a moment: "But what if I don't own the business or am not involved in the top management leadership decisions? How do I make real changes that will affect what it is we do?"

If you're not in charge of *everything*, you're certainly in charge of *something*. Out of the tiny acorn the mighty oak grows and so forth. You probably have more control over operations, outputs, people, results, and most importantly, the care and welfare of customers, than you may first realize. Let this book help you find your place in your organization and show you the steps to follow to change what you can and not worry about what you can't.

I hope this book will appeal to small-business owners and like-minded entrepreneurs, risk takers, leaders, hard workers, and the worriers and the doers, whose emotions and blood pressure are tied directly to the success or failure of their businesses. The motivators of these people—and there are many—start and end with their desire to keep the doors open another day, using brains, guts, and that other less talked about but equally important small-business success factor, a little luck.

Although Woody Allen has so accurately said, "Half of success in life is just showing up," it helps to show up and be in the right place at the right time. Some might call it fate or more accurately, the product of very hard work, but sometimes real success in your small business will come when you least expect it.

But instead of waiting for a miracle that might never come, start investing your time and talent into inputs, outcomes, and results. What you put into your small business is what you get out of it.

A brief discussion of this book's format is now in order. In the interest of clarity, reader comprehension, and ease of writing, I've designed certain parts of this book in an "ask it and answer it" fashion. Because many small-business owners have similar worries, fears, and apprehensions about what it means to be truly "service-driven," I often use the rhetorical question format to address the common questions I've heard, had asked of me, or discovered through my own reading, research, and writing about this subject.

Further, I'm not naive enough to believe that you'll pick up this book, begin at page one, and read all the way through to the end without stopping. Although this would be indeed commendable, life and work can interfere with your desire to read uninterrupted, so I know it's not always possible.

By using this question-answer writing design from time to time, I'm also giving you the opportunity to pick the book up, read some, put it back down, and come back to it, all without losing too much of your train of thought.

And if it appears that the name "Karl Albrecht" creeps into these pages with some frequency, that's no accident either. I have the benefit of being related by blood to the man known throughout the world as the "dean of the service management concept." My father's collected ideas about the management of service quality and customer value has filled a number of bestselling books over the last ten years. Since I cut my teeth on this subject at his knee, it's only fair for the student to credit the professor.

Much of my father's influence as the calm eye in the service management hurricane has come from his ability to communicate his message to CEOs, top executives, and to senior management in companies all around the world. Rather than just repeating what he has done, I've tried to aim my message at what I feel is an underrepresented part of the service management revolution—the small-business owner, operator, executive, manager, and supervisor.

Having worked for small businesses, managed them, and even owned them, I feel well-qualified to mix what I have learned from service experts like my father and other authors, management consultants, and small-business experts around the country and the world with my own experiences as a member of the small business marketplace.

Small businesses are hardly static. If you had been in business twenty years ago, your firm might have been the only one of its kind selling products or services to new customers who hungrily leaped at the chance to buy them.

Now with a competitor literally on every corner, you may have to compete constantly with another small business that sells the same product or service as you do. What used to be easy one or two decades ago, is now hard. The single driving factor that can differentiate you from the guy across the street is not price or value or the words "new and improved" on your box, it's in the way you treat the customer who comes through the front door.

Think of your own buying habits. Do you shop at stores or patronize service businesses that may be higher priced rather than other cheaper, closer places? You probably do so because the people who work there treat you better. You're not alone. Your customers—potential, new, or current—think that way too.

I hope you find this book worthy of not just reading, but re-reading. Changing the way you do business, even if it's all for the better, takes time, energy, motivation, and a lasting commitment to finish what you've started. As a member of the thriving small-business community, you've already demonstrated admirably that you can change on demand.

Consider this book your signal to move out smartly.

—STEVE ALBRECHT
San Diego, California
August 1994

Chapter 1

The Customer Obsession: The Mission Statement

"If you want to truly understand something, try to change it."

—KURT LEWIN

If you're like most small-business owners, operators, executives, or managers, you're probably reading this book over a quick lunchtime sandwich, in between meetings, or on a bumpy or crowded airplane, en route back home after a visit to a client's office.

Tempus fugit. Or, if you're like me and never studied Latin in parochial school, "Time is fleeting." Next to people and money, time is one of the hardest things we manage. If your small business has been in operation for three or more years (the so-called rule of thumb for long-term survivability) and it's going great guns, then you have precious little of this slippery substance to waste.

A quote from the *Corporate Growth Report* illustrates this best, albeit with some painful visual imagery:

Every morning in Africa, a gazelle wakes up. It knows that it must run faster than the fastest lion or it will be killed. Every morning a lion wakes up. It knows it must outrun the slowest gazelle or it will starve to death. It doesn't matter whether you're a lion or a gazelle: When the sun comes up, you'd better be running![1]

While it's easy to understand the spirit of this quotation, it's probably safe to assume that the smart money is bet on the lions. The point is, small-business life is not an idyllic one.

SLAVES TO SMALL-BUSINESS SUCCESS

You're certainly busy meeting the needs of your staff, colleagues, peers, bosses, supervisors, shareholders, board of directors, partners, bankers, suppliers, vendors, marketers, sales people, front-line employees, and behind-the-scenes employees, and when all of them are finally semisatiated after eight, ten, twelve, or sixteen hours in a working day, it's home to your family, pets, or comfy chair.

Guess what? If your small business is less than three years old and in a down mode, if it has seen brighter days, or if it's struggling to keep the doors open, you *still* have the same above-listed commitments, only more so. And handling these commitments, solving the never-ending slew of problems, and still trying to be innovative, creative, and customer-friendly is your challenge. There are always those times when you just want to roll over, go back to bed, and—to quote one weary small-business executive who has fought many a battle in his time—"just mail it in for the day."

No matter where you are on the small-business success scale, things are never too easy. While TV commercials like to show the entrepreneurial businessperson faxing an important memo to colleagues from the sandy beaches of Hawaii or E-mailing important missives to clients from a book-lined study in the countryside summer house, the reality is that you're on the move—mentally or physically—from the time you arrive at work until the time you head home.

Take a quick look back at the list of people and entities who demand your constant attention. What's missing? Or, more important, *who's* missing? *The customers.* Did you catch the deliberate omission of these VIP's from the list? If not, don't get discouraged. It's all a part of how you were trained as a Western businessperson. Most of us were trained to focus on outcomes and results, people and problems. Get this done first, get that done next, and so on. Too many businesspeople still see the needs of the customer as some sort of relative inconvenience that gets in the way of out-come-based business management. Under the stress of too much paperwork, not enough time, or too many problems, complaints, or mistakes, it's not uncommon to hear the following incredible phrase spoken: "You know, this would be a great place to work if it wasn't for all these damned customers taking up our time."

Think of your own world. Do you spend the majority of your time planning for the future or putting out forest fires that flare up in your plant, store, or office? Do you schedule several hours each day just to tip your chair back, prop your feet up, and think about long-term goals or new and better ways to run your company, department, division, or group? Are you paid to stay at home, stare off into the distance, and dictate some new methods, systems, policies, and procedures for corporate growth into your tape recorder?

Before you can answer any of these blue-sky questions, you're probably reaching for your helmet, asbestos raincoat, and water-proof boots. You're already heading down the hall with your axe, hose, and Dalmatian dog at the ready.

If you failed to see the absence of the customer in your list of small-business duties, could it be that your fireproof hood has slipped over your eyes as you race from one calamity to the next?

THE SMALL-BUSINESS OWNER'S BUG LIST

Psychologists and other stress-management experts often advise people who feel like the walls are closing in to write down what they call a "bug list." Sometimes it helps to see your problems on paper, where they either don't look so bad or at least look more manageable. And the bug list is not for small things like "Don't like wife's pot roast" or "Car is running funny." The true bug list should cover major problems, areas, or current catastrophes that need fixing. We can take this idea over to the small-business arena. If you were to stop a finite number of small-business owners and ask them to make out a bug list of their top concerns, most of them probably would look like this one.

Small-Business Owner Bug List

This is a general compendium of worries, frustrations, problems, and other everyday short- or long-term headaches that bug the average small-business owner, followed by a discussion of what makes them buglike. To phrase it another way, "What are the things about your small business that keep you from sleeping soundly at night?"

Capital—*where to get it; how to keep it.*

This is first on the bug list for obvious reasons. Anybody who doesn't really believe that money makes the world go round has never worked as a small-businessperson. Wherever you are on the small-business evolutionary scale—whether startup or long-time and going concern—you know by now that Cash is King. Money keeps the doors open, whether you began operations last month or ten years ago. And while you shouldn't get obsessed with it, you'd better give the subject of funds your constant attention.

Studies of small-business failures point to the same pattern: Most good businesses that go bankrupt or shut down do so because they are or were undercapitalized. You can have the greatest product, offer the best services imaginable, and treat your customers like the golden geese they are, but if you don't have enough money, you're history.

I'm reminded of a colleague who started a specialty magazine, which is always a difficult go in any economy. With eight months of issues under his belt, he was actually starting to see the potential for a profit. He had landed several large and well-known national advertising accounts and was truly poised for greatness. But before the champagne had stopped fizzing, he received a polite phone call from his investor group—the money people who had backed his magazine from the start. "Sorry, we need the loss as a write-off for our corporate taxes. We're pulling the plug on you. Adios."

And money struggles, which dredge up plenty of problems anyway, can interfere with your need, desire, or ability to provide the kind of high-quality service to your customers that will keep them coming back in the first place. If you've been involved with businesses that have imploded from within or exploded from without, you probably can quote stories of customer nightmares where any inkling of service quality vanished into thin air as the organization struggled, slipped, or sank.

Debt—*How to lower it; how to get into it carefully.*

Isn't it curious that when some huge and well-known company takes a bath on some questionable bond investment, merger mistake, or poison-pill fight, and winds up in debt to the tune of eleventy-billion (that's with a B) dollars, the business and finance magazines and the bankers refer to this as "manageable debt," a "high debt ratio," or a "strong debt position"?

But if your firm were to get into debt at something more like the five- or six-figure level, those same magazines and bankers would shake their heads warily, rub their collective chins, and say your small business was "in over its head," "overleveraged," or "debt-laden."

It could be all a question of perspective, but as one outraged small-business owner has complained to all who will listen, "How come my bank will write billions in loans at the drop of a hat to an overseas Third World country that won't even be able to pay back the interest and it takes me six months and a forest of paperwork to get a simple line of credit for my company?"

These days, debt is something you should want your competitor to have. Even though the hard-charging, shoot-'em-up 1980s are over, the debt generated by thousands of companies, large and small, during that "me" decade continues to cling to balance sheets across the land. Getting into big debt used to be fun, when there were piles of money on the horizon and the economic forecast looked as rosy as a ripe peach. Now, with the peach eaten and many companies left holding the pit, heavy debt is back to being its usual ogrelike self.

According to a September 1993 *Wall Street Journal* article, reducing company debt has become a major priority at many smaller firms.

> The debt-shunning entrepreneur has plenty of company. As bank loan rates are the lowest in two decades, one might expect to see small businesses rushing out to borrow, borrow, borrow. But the reverse seems to be true: Many small companies are rushing to pay off debt. Numerous small-business owners fear that the current tepid economic recovery won't last. Then, as profits decline, even low-cost debt would shackle them with interest payments, onerous bank imposed loan restrictions and threats to their personal assets required as collateral, all of which become more burdensome in tough times. Many small companies, of course, have fewer resources than large concerns to weather the effects of a downturn, and thus are particularly prone to worry.[2]

In other words, money is a charter member of the bug list.

Taxes—*how to legally avoid, defer, or lessen them. (For answers to where to come up with the money to pay them in the first place, see the previous sections.)*

If your firm is making more money than last year and paying less in taxes, either check to see that your accountant is not in a Bolivian hideaway avoiding IRS extradition, or give him or her a nice raise. It's more probable that you're paying more in taxes no matter how well or how poorly your company performed. "The government," to quote a line from the 1987 movie comedy *Raising Arizona*, "she do take a bite."

The reason this item is on so many small-business bug lists is simple: People feel like they're damned if they do and damned if they don't.

"If our firm makes good money," goes the complaint, "it all seems to go out to the government in new tax brackets, late paperwork fines, assessments, one-time charges, state taxes, local taxes, and business license fees. If we lose money, we still have to pay through the nose. It's almost like there's no incentive to succeed, and it's almost less expensive to go out of business. We make just enough money to stay open. Why does the government always seem to have one foot pressed firmly on our backs?"

Sound familiar? The cost of staying in business is getting higher by the day. And with massive changes coming in everything from health care and labor laws to the tax code, don't look for much help from your benevolent Uncle Sam. Of course, it could be worse. As Will Rogers put it, "Just be glad you're not getting all the government you're paying for."

Paperwork—*how to lessen it, delegate it, or avoid it.*

The paperless society is far from being just around the corner. In, say, another two centuries, we just might get it perfected and on-line, but for now, there's probably at least a ream of foolscap on your desk at any given moment.

Someone, somewhere, wants a piece of paper from you and wants it yesterday. If it's not a government regulatory agency or an irate personnel manager, it's an employee, your secretary, someone above or below you in the chain of command, or, it's safe to say, a customer.

The woods are full of time-managing, paper-free, organized-to-the-max consultants who would be happy to come into your company and teach you and yours how to be safe and sane paper pushers. Now, if you could just find their brochure among all that stuff on your desk, credenza, bulletin board, in-or-out box, and file cabinet.

Employees—*how to hire good ones, keep them, and manage them safely and effectively; how to motivate managers and supervisors, and provide a positive example for everyone who works here.*

Most small-business owners are intelligent enough to know that they cannot possibly run every facet of their business. If they are to succeed at any level, they'll require the services and expertise of good help. Yet, even as most of them nod and admit that they must delegate responsibilities and assignments to their employees, it's still hard to let go.

"I built this company from the ground up," says one owner, "and now you're asking me to let my baby go play with razor blades?"

This kind of thinking is common, even in the smoothest-running organizations. And it's why death and disability from overwork and overworry are still the hallmarks of the small-business owner.

Systems—*how and where to fix the way we do things (some of them wrong) around here.*

We'll discuss the need for effective service systems throughout this book. As you stroll the grounds of your company, watching people work and interact with one another, with your customers, and with the actual products or services you offer, you should be able to see most of what works right and what doesn't.

Some systems problems are easy to spot because they are so glaring. But some businesspeople refuse to see them even though they're more than obvious. As an example, if your telephone system hung up on the customer after one and a half rings, failed to answer past the stroke of 2:00 p.m. each day, exchanged lines, mixed conversations around the building, or otherwise failed to perform in a professional manner, you'd jump to change it. Out with the old and in with the new, right away.

So why is it that you can see the same kinds of *systems* problems in the ways in which your organization conducts business with your customers and yet still not be quick to make the same necessary changes? The answers are many and all-consuming, but at this junction box in our story, suffice it to say that it's often harder to fix what's already been broken than to start fresh with a new approach. Sometimes you'll just have to bite the bullet—in terms of costs, time, and headaches—and make the necessary changes.

Strategy—*how to change the fact that we seem to be going in different directions instead of working as a team.*

The subject of strategy is a deep one. It ranges from the esoteric and the ethereal to the hard-nosed and concrete, with several stops along the way. Just as systems look at the *way* you do business, your strategy looks at the *why* you do business.

When the weary small-businessperson sits down at the end of another brutal day and asks, either out loud or silently, "What business are we *really* in?" you're seeing a strategy crisis.

In case you didn't see your favorite bug list item or are a glutton for more, consider these candidates as well:

- Problems with our products or services that need constant attention
- How to compete in our market in this tough economy
- Rising costs for our labor, product development, manufacturing, distribution, advertising, marketing, employee benefits, etc.
- Competitive pressure—at home and abroad
- Where to get the money to pay for the coming changes in health care, employment taxes, minimum wage increases, and income taxes

And lastly, a perennial bug list favorite:

- Civil suits

Here's a guaranteed heartburn-starter: Over 95 percent of 240 small-business owners surveyed by the American Institute of Certified Public Accountants said that "frivolous" lawsuits are on the rise, and 70 percent said that their liability-related expenses, such as insurance premiums and defense costs, have increased over the past five years. Companies that had never dreamed of even having an attorney on retainer now have one working with them in their building.

What the bug list helps to illustrate is that we spend the vast majority of our time as owners, leaders, executives, managers, and supervisors handling the large and small problems, opportunities, and puzzles that arise each day. Thinking about the future, if it is done at all, is usually an on-the-run process at best.

TAKING THE CUSTOMER FOR GRANTED

If we agree from the outset that customers are the lifeblood of any organization (and especially for the small business, which has even less room for error), how can we justify the operational stance that says, "We'll get to them later"? How can we fail to notice that the health and happiness of our business relies on commerce, the exchange of *their* money for *our* goods and services?

In a phrase, it's because we really do take these people, as nearer-to-God-than-thee and important as they are, for granted. Notice that my earlier description of your small business specified more than three years of operation. If you are in this category, think back a bit. For the first year, the customer was all you ever thought about. "How do we get more business? We need to market ourselves, call people, sell, advertise, sell, look for new customers, sell, deliver our products or services, sell, and sell, and sell."

If your company managed (literally and figuratively) to survive the first year—and, as many business reporters like to point out, well over half of all undercapitalized small-business start-ups don't make it past their one-year anniversaries—things didn't change much. You still spend your second year digging for new customers. However, you probably also took on other responsibilities, like employees, paperwork, taxes and finances, human resource duties, inventory, and asset management. The search for the golden customer was still a top priority, but if you were lucky enough to begin to break even or make a profit, other management issues crept into your sphere of control. Suddenly, or maybe gradually, the care and feeding of the customer was not your first responsibility.

Some customers came and stayed, others came and went, and

still others sat in your doorway, waiting to be invited, pulled, or led in to conduct business with you.

If, by your third year in operation, you were saddled with even more responsibilities, and the ways of meeting the needs, desires, expectations, and aspirations of your customers may have fallen into someone else's hands, or become the sole assignment of someone or something called the ever-popular Customer Service Department.

A television commercial for one of this country's largest airlines played out this same evolution in a real-time fashion.

Standing at the head of a large room filled with his managers, the chief executive of his company lamented that its largest customer had just fired it for failing to meet its needs. Wearing a pained expression, the CEO said in essence, "And I don't blame them. We used to help our customers face to face. Now we do business with fax machines, voice mail and 'have your people get back to our people.' We've lost sight of who is important to our success."

Handing out an inch-thick stack of airline tickets, the leader ordered his people back out on to the road and en route to new meetings with their existing or former customers. The message built into this thirty-second homily is clear: "We've gotten too big for our own britches. It's time to get back to our company's basic strategic philosophy, mission, and message: It's the customer."

With that in mind, let's prove why excellence in service quality should be the foundation for all you do now, and all you will do in the future.

A REAL WORKING DEFINITION OF SERVICE QUALITY

➤ *Isn't the phrase "service quality" a fairly abstract concept? How do you define such a broad category?*

Some business cynics might argue that the words *service* and *quality* go together about as well as other oxymorons like *jumbo shrimp*, *affordable housing*, or *honest politicians*.

While it's true that the words *service* and *quality* are loaded with possibilities, it is possible to narrow our view of them into the following working definition. This mission statement will carry us through the remainder of this book.

Quality service is what our company must provide, through the careful management of our strategies, systems, and people to meet and often exceed the needs and expectations of our current and new external and internal customers. By creating a service-driven organization, we can capture more market share, offer more value than our competitors, and establish a workplace environment that is profitable, healthy, and beneficial to everyone who works with it and for it.

If you are to consider your organization truly customer-focused, this mission statement must become a part of your corporate credo. Whether you use these exact words or not is immaterial. What is important is that some form of this same strong message must be communicated to all members of your organization.

Obviously, if you're in charge of everything and everyone, you can make a lot of waves until everyone from the top on down has heard this message and, if not taken it completely to heart, at least understood its significance in terms of the health of the company.

Let's look at each part of this mission statement in detail.

➤ *How do we create the "strategies and systems" to help our people work in a more customer-focused manner?*

We can define service strategies as the "distinctive formulas, approaches, or principles for delivering service quality that are both important to the customer and deliverable by the organization." Put even more simply, the only way to figure out how to better serve the customers is to ask them what they want and give it to them.

And the way we implement service strategies is through the careful creation of service systems. If every customer who comes into your store tells you, "I want to be able to pay with a credit card," then you had better develop a strategy that says, "Use your credit card here!" You had better set about creating a system to help your front-line employees easily and efficiently accept customer credit cards.

Your overall service *strategy*, which can change as necessary, should guide the people in your organization to use customer-friendly *systems* to meet their own needs and the needs of the customer.

Why is it important for the service *employee* to like your systems, know your systems, and be able to use your systems? Because he or she is usually face to face with the customer at the "moment of truth." A newfangled computerized credit card approval system that forces the customer and the employees to twiddle their collective thumbs for ten minutes quashes the needs of either party. At this critical moment of truth, the customer makes a value judgment about you and your organization.

DEFINING MOMENTS OF TRUTH

➤ *Tell me more about this "moment of truth" idea. I've heard the phrase used a lot lately. What does it mean exactly?*

This service term is not new, but many businesspeople have still failed to grasp its vast significance. Coined by service management guru Jan Carlzon, the former CEO of European airline Scandinavian Air Services (SAS), a "moment of truth" or "MOT" can offer you a powerful wake-up call about the state of your service business.

As Carlzon described it, as far back as the early 1980s, a *moment of truth* is:

Any episode where a customer comes into contact with any aspect of your company, no matter how distant, and by this contact, has an opportunity to form an opinion about your company.

And moments of truth, both positively and negatively, are taking place around your organization each day. Some of them may please you, and others may horrify you.

When a customer comes into your hardware store and sees two of your salespeople eating at the cash register, engaged in a lengthy and uninterruptable conversation about sports, and in no real hurry to offer a hint of service, you've just seen a moment of truth come and (as the customer will probably do) go.

Just because I used a negative MOT first doesn't mean that plenty of swell ones don't exist. And not every MOT requires human interaction between customer and employee. When the customer comes into the lobby of your factory and sees a neat and clean foyer area, comfy chairs, an inviting coffeepot, and fresh and current magazines, he or she makes an immediate positive evaluation of the people who work there and the company itself.

If, to continue, this person is greeted by a friendly receptionist, offered a cup of that fine-looking coffee, and told to have a seat in a soft chair while he or she waits, then these subsequent moments of truth add to the customer's overall feeling of satisfaction, ease, or comfort.

This simple service idea is captured in the moment of truth concept, yet too many small-business owners, managers, and supervisors get so caught up in their duties that they fail to recognize the moments of truth going on—either blatantly obvious or hidden beneath the surface—right in front of their eyes.

Good, positive, helpful, shining, or even out-of-the-ordinary moments of truth mean you'll probably get high marks on the customer's mental report card. And you can guess what bad, negative, harmful, dull, or below-standard MOTs mean for your score on that same report card—a failing grade that may even be well deserved.

➤ *So how do we control these moments of truth and get a good grade?*

It is in fact possible to *manage* the moments of truth and come away with more than passing marks from your ever-alert customers. In fact, there's the rub: Becoming a customer-powered business literally *starts* with your understanding of what your company's moments of truth are, and how you can change or remove the bad ones and make the good ones even better.

By understanding first how and when these events are taking place in your company, you can start to see where changes—immediate or long-term—need to be made.

DEFINING YOUR CUSTOMERS

➤ *What about the part of the service mission definition that speaks about current and new customers?*

One of the initial mistakes small-businesspeople make about the concept of service management involves their understanding of who and *where* their customers really are. Some descriptions will help you identify them:

> **current customers**—are the customers who do business with your firm now. They have bought your products and services in the recent or distant past and continue to do so on a regular or irregular basis. Their presence in and around your company may be the result of accident, advertising, direct mail, location, word of mouth, referral, price, value, history, service excellence, or luck.
>
> If you run a chain of convenience stores, you may see them every morning as they buy coffee and snacks. If you own a car dealership, you may see them every two, three,

or five years. If you own a computer hardware company, you may see them each time you come out with a new product.

Their presence inside and outside your organization can serve as a comfort, even indirectly, since these are the folks who help you to pay your bills, pay your employees, and keep your doors open.

You may be highly aware of their needs and spend time actively trying to fulfil or exceed their expectations. Or you may not be aware of their needs and have to try to guess accurately how to keep them happy.

A satisfied customer is not just one who comes back to do business with you again, but one who is happy to make that choice. This distinction becomes clearer when you consider that most people don't have a whit of choice in where they get their electricity service, cable TV service, household water and sewer services, or city telephone service. The companies who so generously allow us to use these services are usually monopolies, and therefore we *have* to do business with them if we want what they offer.

If people *have* to do business with your firm, consider yourself lucky. Chances are, they don't. It's up to you and the people in your organization to make them so happy that they almost feel that they need to come to you just to get the good treatment, as well as the goods or services, they always want.

new customers—are just coming into contact with your firm for the first or second time.

If you operate a printing company, they may be at the order desk, dropping off a critical project for the first time with you. Theirs might be the first load your trucking company hauls out of the warehouse. They are standing in line at your cash registers, holding their purchases and waiting to pay. They are dialing the phone in response to your Yellow Pages ad, your brochure, or your direct-mail piece, or following the recommendation of a friend. They are waiting to be seated at your restaurant. They are installing your software for the first time.

Wherever and whoever they are, we know one thing: They feel vulnerable.

➤ *Vulnerable? About what?*

Put yourself in their shoes. Trying new things makes most people somewhat apprehensive. If you don't believe this, ask yourself how many times in the last month you ate lunch at a new restaurant. Once? Three times? Not at all? How come?

People are largely creatures of habit and slaves to routine. We get comfortable eating in the same places, shopping in the same places, and doing business with those firms that offer a level of service that is better than passable and that often meets or exceeds our highest expectations.

Going into your new retail store, doctor's office, restaurant, or other walk-in, drive-up, or phone-it-in business is a leap of faith. People come in with a certain expectation of treatment. This expectation gets put on the line every time they try something new.

Hence the concept of the moment of truth becomes even more critical with this new and vulnerable customer. The well-established or less hypercritical customer may accept a little missing paint, a systems screwup, or an atypically surly employee. The new customer, who has his or her MOT detector on full radar alert from the initial contact until the end, may not be so forgiving.

➤ *So what is the difference between "external" and "internal" customers?*

This concept is critical to your understanding of who your customers really are. Before you can make the sweeping changes necessary to turn your organization into a customer-driven entity, you must know who is who.

You can recognize *external customers* immediately. They are the paying customers who come to your company from the outside. They have responded to your business presence in some fashion or another, and they have arrived at your doorstep, telephone line, or mailbox ready to exchange their money for your goods or services. The person who registers at a hotel is involved in an external customer relationship with the desk clerk. Cashing your paycheck at your bank involves an external customer relationship between you and the teller (unless, of course, you work for the bank as well, which leads us to the discussion of internal customer relationships).

The definition of the *internal customers,* who are not so obvious but are abundant in every organization, requires a bit more thought. These are the people who *work* in your organization and do business with *each other.*

And while most small-businesspeople can easily identify the many thousands of external customer relationships—and, with some thought, the accompanying moments of truth—going on every day in their own organizations, they often fail to notice the internal ones. People who work for and with you have internal customers all around them. To the people who work in your payroll department, the entire company is their customer. The man who delivers the interoffice mail has a whole roomful of customers. The woman who answers your telephone order lines is served by your people in the shipping department, the billing center, and the creators of your mail-order catalogs.

It's easy to overlook these ongoing internal relationships inside your own firm because, for one thing, they've always existed. "I know all about these interactions between our employees," the harried business owner says. "I pay my people to do their work and my managers and supervisors to make sure things run smoothly. I've got to spend my time more productively, getting and keeping my customers."

True, up to a point. Looking outside your company at the needs of the customers is perfectly acceptable and in fact necessary for your survival; however, failing to see that the "inside" customers must have their needs met and managed is foolhardy. The people who do the day-to-day work inside your organization follow certain systems, methods, techniques, and operations to get their jobs done.

How and where they learned these techniques is largely based on—in the worst cases—trial and error, accidental discovery, shortcuts, or word-of-mouth, or (in the best cases) help from veteran employees or supervisors, on-the-job training, or pointed and humane direction from their supervisors, managers, or other company leaders. Or in other instances it may be a combination of the best and worst ways to achieve some desired outcome.

The point is that these systems procedures either help or hinder the way your internal customers do their jobs and, ultimately, the way they serve their own internal *and* external customers.

One of the strongest messages to come out of Karl Albrecht's best-selling 1985 book *Service America!* was this simple but effective way to describe the ultimate internal customer relationship:

If you're not serving the customer, you'd better be serving someone who is.[3]

Take these thirteen simple words, aim them at any internal customer relationship in your company, and see what appears in the sights. The remainder of this book will focus on identifying not only the things that the external customer thinks are critically important, but also some of the systems and strategies you must create to streamline and improve the way your internal customers serve one another along with their external customers.

Positive and negative examples of this abound. As you look about your own firm, keep two interrelated things in mind:

1. Does the way we do business with one another here affect the way we do business with our customers?

2. If we can help one another to get our collective work done, will that improve the way we take care of the external customers? Conversely, if we constantly fight, backbite, and stall, hinder, and abuse one another with poorly designed systems, bad employees, and bad management on the inside, will we ultimately hurt the way we do business with our customers?

The answers to these questions are yes, yes, and yes. It's fine to want to climb up into the crow's nest and look for the customer on the horizon. But any organization that wants to serve the customer must start by making sure that the people who are steering, fueling, and cleaning the boat are having their own needs met.

The on-line telephone technical support people who are engaged in a long-running battle with the software engineers about the design of your product can't help but let this feud interfere with the way they answer customers' software questions.

The front-line counter clerk who can't get any help from the Parts Department, Shipping and Receiving, or Purchasing will definitely not want to take the full blame when a customer comes in steaming mad after an error.

So you can see that the way we treat one another on the inside has a lot to do with how we treat the customer coming from the outside. Customers who come to you with the same problems may actually be helping you recognize some internal customer conflicts that you haven't seen yet.

➤ *What about the last parts of the service mission definition? How can we get more market-share, offer more value than our competitors, and create a workplace that's good for our customers, employees, partners, and shareholders?*

This is certainly a tall order, but it's not unobtainable, especially since each of these elements tends to go hand in glove with the others. One of the predominant factors in increasing market share is customer satisfaction, right? And offering more value to your customers than your competitors offers leads to higher customer satisfaction (and more market share, to continue the theme a bit more).

And you create a workplace that's good for your customers, employees, partners, and shareholders when you address the needs of each. And it is possible to meet or exceed the needs of each of these highly divergent groups and still not end up in the tall grass.

By providing your employees with a safe, humane, and relatively comfortable working environment, nurturing their successes, gently but firmly correcting their mistakes, and managing by positive example instead of by the old whip-and-chair method, you can create a healthy, nourishing place to work. Isn't it possible and even likely that this will rub off on the customers as well? Have you ever heard of a company that was a truly terrible place to work, and yet served its customers with style, grace, and flair? Not likely.

SERVICE AS AN OBSESSION

➤ *Is it really possible for a firm to be obsessed with its customers?*

It had better be. The dictionary defines *obsession* as a "ruling idea or a mania," and you could certainly argue that the best service companies, those that are truly service-driven, border on the maniacal in their commitment to their customers.

But while our mission statement definition offers you a good model, it's also not easy to achieve. Thinking about it won't make it happen. There is a long and even arduous journey from the statement "Our company needs to focus more on the customer" to "We are truly a service-driven firm."

➤ *Do the customers really notice this obsession? Or do they just take it for granted when things go well?*

In large part, this last question is answered with a solid, "It's true." Thanks to the continued expansion of the customer-oriented service management revolution, what used to be called basic service— in a restaurant, clean plates, edible food, and passable service from the wait staff—now is no longer acceptable as even a minimum standard. People now require, and in fact demand, higher levels of so-called minimum service—spotless plates, superb food, and sparkling table service.

The hotel industry, with its now-standard free shampoos, mints on pillows, free buffets, et al., has helped to create its own monster. What used to be thought of as a perk—"Oh look! A free shoe horn and a shower cap!"—is now as common in even the most pedestrian hotels as scratchy bath towels.

Many people who stay in hotels have come to see these items as basic services. Consequently, if they were to go to a hotel that *didn't* offer a mint on the pillow, mouthwash in eight designer flavors, or decaffeinated double dutch chocolate coffee, they would feel somewhat ill used. "I get those things when I go to other hotels," goes the reasoning. "Why not here? What's wrong with this place?"

And whether this displeasure is voiced aloud or silently, it exists. As oddly paradoxical as this all sounds, it's true. By raising the level of basic service and setting new standards, you create a new level of expectations in the customers' eyes.

As a small-business service provider, you have two choices: complain about it or adapt to it. The winners adjust, react, and keep going. The losers gripe, underreact, and stay put.

Among a myriad of other things, small-business survival is also about adaptation and the changes you'll need to make to persevere. This is not an accidental, apathetic, or wait-and-see approach. You cannot afford to wait for things to change. You have to decide how to change, when to change, and how often to change the changes. In short, your ability to thrive as a small business first depends upon your being aware and flexible.

New York Knicks basketball coach Pat Riley, a great motivator of himself and others, offers this thought to reinforce the need for you to act wisely and immediately:

You have to learn to take a hit and to recover. My wife, Chris, and I took a great canoe trip in the Grand Canyon last year. Before we set off, our guide told us there were two rules to follow: "First, you have to wear a life vest. Second, you are definitely at some point going to fall into the water and wind up underneath the boat. When you do, you have to become a participant in your own recovery."

It's time to put on your life vest and get ready for the trip down the river of small-business service-quality success. Rough or smooth, you'll get wet, but at least you'll get to make the decisions about which way to steer the boat.

Notes

1. Reprinted from *Reader's Digest*, April 1993, 240.

2. "Reducing Debt Is Top Priority at Small Firms," *Wall Street Journal*, Sept. 8, 1993, B1.

3. Karl Albrecht and Ron Zemke, *Service America!: Doing Business in the New Economy* (Homewood, Ill.: Dow Jones-Irwin, 1985), 106.

4. Roger Rosenblatt, "Taking the Man Inside," *Men's Journal*, Nov. 1993, 26.

Chapter 2

Success Obstacles: Why Even the Big Guys Fail

"Frustration is when the same snow that covers the
ski slopes makes the roads to them impassable."
—JAMES HOLT McGAVRAN

These days, stories of failed service programs abound. From front-line "smile-training" classes that succeed only in creating animosity in the employees to supposed "customer-friendly" systems that only make things harder for the customer and tougher for the employee, there is no shortage of false starts, weak attempts, and total failures.

This chapter focuses on some of the distractions, misguided movements, failings, and old Total Quality Management (TQM) mindsets that can send many otherwise solid service programs spinning toward the scrap pile.

Many big companies are like bad cameras—that is, they have *focus* problems. They can't isolate or coordinate their business activities along one single theme. They create boundless customer service plans, they have all the right motivations and the best intentions, but then they go off like a shotgun, spraying people, assets, resources, inventory, and strategies in a million different directions.

Some firms have no focus, others forget their focus, still others change their focus too often and thereby screw up already smooth-running operations, and others, worse yet, jump off winning service programs before they get halfway around the track. And last, one of the most common problems is companies that fail to change their focus when situations, or, more importantly, the customer, demands it.

THE SLEEPING SHARK: MOVE OR DIE

The dramatic changes in market share for IBM over the last five years have left Big Blue feeling more like Big Sad and Blue. "The personal computer?" the IBM folks in Rochester, New York, and Boca Raton, Florida, said aloud. "Oh, sure, we'll make 'em like everybody else, but we shouldn't forget that we created the whole darn computer industry with the mainframe. The mainframe got us here, and by God, the mainframe will take us where we want to go."

History can be a cruel teacher. Even a giant conglomerate like IBM can get handed a nasty surprise. As the late 1980s and early 1990s have shown us, the computer-buying customer shifted his or her interest away from the bulky mainframe to the more manageable PC.

Looking at IBM, many customers asked, "Why buy one room-sized mainframe computer when, for way less money, we can buy a whole roomful of personal computers and link them together into a network?"

As IBM's continuously slipping market share has attested, other smaller personal computer companies heard this clarion call long before IBM did and decided to answer it. Too bad IBM can't get paid a royalty every time someone in business, retail, or the media uses the term "IBM clone." It must puzzle the personnel at IBM to see a device they helped to bring to the market—the personal computer—get copied, recopied, and re-recopied one thousand and ten times over by smaller companies with less money, less clout, and certainly less advertising expenses.

What these smaller firms may have lacked in bucks or influence, they made up for with marketing savvy, a more intense focus on the needs of the customer, and no small amount of good timing.

Dell Computer's rise as an IBM-clone superpower is well known in small-business success circles. Founder Michael Dell realized as early as his college years that he could make money selling IBM-clone computers via mail order. What started as a small-time operation has grown to a multimillion-dollar organization. Dell had the foresight to look at the market situation, see who was filling customer needs and who wasn't, and dive into the fray with his own ideas.

And Dell is far from the only hero in the PC wars. Canon, AST, AT&T, Zenith, Hewlett-Packard, Packard Bell, Radio Shack/Tandy, Epson, NEC, Toshiba, and literally scores of other off-brand computer hardware manufacturers have their own machines that they sell either directly under their own brand name or to other companies for relicensing. Did their good fortune come by walking across bricks already paved by IBM? Yes and no. IBM certainly brought the personal computer out of the labs and homes of the "micro-nerds" and into the office, but it failed to see, as others did, the vast significance of the PC in the years to come.

Its company lifeblood had always been the mainframe, and it saw no reason to jump off a steed that was way ahead of the pack. Trouble was, the other horses behind it switched tracks entirely and began running in a completely different direction.

In the biblical story of David versus Goliath, the big man was felled by a single stone. IBM has taken a pile of stones to its collective forehead, but while it may have staggered and even gone down on one knee, it's hardly about to go out of business.

Some lessons, like the bright idea that says, "We should diversify and give our old and new customers what they really want, rather than what we think they're supposed to have," take time to learn.

LEARNING FROM THE BIG GUYS

Any book about small-business success will be filled with stories of large businesses that once were small and have now survived and thrived. These literary comparisons are inevitable, and yet they serve a purpose. We can learn from the wisdom or mistakes of the high rollers—and there have been countless examples of both—and use this information to our advantage.

If you run a small photo-processing factory, the trick is to see yourself in competition not with Kodak or Fuji, but with the guy down the road or across town or across the city who also runs a business like yours. The beauty of small-business operations is that you can compete on a number of different levels that your much larger counterparts cannot.

Think of your own day-to-day operations. If you employ fifteen people in your retail store, you can make instantaneous changes in procedures in a matter of hours or days. A large business that employs 15,000 people could take months to change something that you could change with a short announcement, a memo, or a phone call.

You have the ability to reach your people right now and make adjustments or improvements in systems, operations, and techniques immediately. Whereas Disneyland has over 300 different employee policy and procedures manuals, you may have only one. And depending upon the size and nature of your company, it may not cover more than twenty pages. And while it may take Federal Express two months to change one of its operational procedures, you might be able to make such a change in two minutes. Size is good, especially if you're a football player or a freight train, but agility can be just as important as girth.

To continue with the David and Goliath analogy, the trick is to have more than one stone at the ready; To paraphrase a popular scatological bumper sticker, Misses Happen. It's not necessary to attack the big guys head on. You just need to be better at the things they can't or won't do for the customer.

▶ *My company just makes things. We know who our customers are, and it's a finite number. We aren't in the service business, we're in the manufacturing business. Right?*

It's time to face some facts. Some people and their firms have gone kicking and screaming into our new service economy. "What about manufacturing?" went up the cry. "We build things for America! We're creators of jobs! We're kings of industry!"

True, up to a point. A company like U.S. Steel, long a stalwart in the fire and foundry days of our Industrial Revolution, does make things out of steel. "Steel is not a service! It's a hard, durable good! We're not in the steel 'service' business! We're in the steel 'production' business!"

Okay, given the huge fall from grace of giant manufacturing companies like U.S. Steel have taken over the years, what can we learn from this manufacturing mindset?

Simply this: You still have to *sell* your product—whatever it is—to someone. Since there are other steel firms in this country, not to mention Japan and Europe, the steel-buying customer has a choice. What many hard-goods manufacturers have still not taken to heart is the undeniable fact that customers want choices; they want to be able to pick who they do business with and, where, why, and how they do business with them.

U.S. Steel is not just in the steel-*production* business, it's in the steel-*providing* business. If I could rewrite part of U.S. Steel's corporate mission statement, I'd say this:

> We create our steel goods for customers who want to build their own products. As such, we should be in the business of giving them the sizes, shapes, designs, and quantities they need to create and complete their ideas. We will work with all of our customers to make sure they can use our products to the best of both of our abilities.

To put it bluntly, it's not what *you* want, it's what the customer wants.

Let's look at the statistics. According to U.S. survey data, about 87 percent of our firms are what might be called "pure" or "near pure" service companies. The remaining 13 percent or so are what might be called "pure" or "near pure" manufacturing organizations. What do these two groups share? They still have customers to serve, no matter what they make, provide, or sell.

➤ *So if McDonald's is now King, how did we move from "smokestacks to the flapjacks" in this country?*

Short question, long answer. Dozens of business books have chronicled our journey from pure industry to pure service. Influences such as the post-World War II baby boom, the rise in disposable income, the availability of the automobile, the advent of television (and advertising), and even the creation of the hamburger and the microchip have led us to where we are.

And our values as a nation have changed. As the buy-and-spend, slash-and-burn 1980s have aptly demonstrated, we *want* things now more than ever before. We want them faster, better, cheaper, and in a variety of 8 different shapes, sizes, fragrances, and textures.

Consumer demand for goods and services is now at a place in our history where it's no longer possible to act like Henry Ford, who could get away with saying, "You can have any color you want, as long as it's black."

In 1837, F. J. Grund said, "It is as if all America were but a giant workshop, over the entrance of which is the blazing inscription, 'No admission here, except on business.'" Well, we're no longer just a giant workshop, we're a giant service machine.

THE SERVICE QUALITY EVOLUTION AND REVOLUTION

➤ *How did this sudden interest in the needs of the customer come about? Haven't we always been serving customers when we sell them our products and services?*

Sadly, no. The idea of the Customers as King did not start with the invention of the motorcar and go forward. And worse yet, as much as we like to say we invented everything, it didn't even begin in the United States.

The now-famous "quality movement" really began as far back as the 1930s, with some work done by three men: Walter Shewhart, W. Edwards Deming, and Joseph Juran. They worked on production and manufacturing concepts and measurement models that had a relatively small influence on American factories and manufacturing entities.

It was not until the years following World War II that Deming and Juran came into their own. In post-war Japan, where they were helping to rebuild the economic infrastructure, their quality-control models were a big success and were adopted by most Japanese manufacturers. And what was popular over there came back over here as the years passed and American businesses looked for ways to compete with the Japanese for product quality and burgeoning market share.

By the 1970s, Philip Crosby joined Deming and Juran to become one of the quality assurance gurus. "Zero defects" was now the goal in all manufacturing processes. These men preached that if you could cut down the number of errors at each stage of production, by statistical definition, you could drastically reduce the number of flaws in the finished product.

By 1980, some businesspeople (not Americans yet, mind you) had begun to look for other ways to measure company efficiency, productivity, and success, by focusing not on how many defect-free widgets they could crank out, but on what the *customers* thought about those widgets and on how to make better widgets to meet the customers' needs and expectations.

Much of this discussion about how to match the company with the customer began in Scandinavia, specifically with Mr. Jan Carlzon, then the CEO of Scandinavian Airlines Service (SAS). At the time, SAS, like other European airlines, was bleeding money from every pore.

To initiate the now-famous financial turnaround of his firm, Carlzon began to teach and preach a concept called *service management*, which put the customers' needs into the majority of the decisions the company made. Suddenly the game had changed, and dramatically.

It wasn't just about how many airplanes they needed to buy, how to get fuel and food and drink and crews on board, and where to send them. Carlzon reasoned that he needed to change the focus of his airline and be critically concerned about what the passenger thought was important. He knew that lower air fares didn't mean much to a customer if the damn plane was always late. And he guessed correctly that it was time for his company to discover what was important to the passengers and give it to them.

By creating an airline that truly was customer-driven (or, more specifically, passenger-driven), Carlzon succeeded in making a huge profit for his organization, even at a time when the other airlines around him continued to founder.

And it wasn't just talk from on high. Carlzon walked his talk by leaving his executive suite and going out to his employees. He initiated a companywide training program for everyone from the next highest executive down to the newest baggage handler. These training seminars, geared for management and the front-line employees, preached the message that serving the needs of the passenger was what was going to save airline. He was right.

Business author and management consultant Karl Albrecht was passing through Europe and Scandinavia at the time and began to hear more and more executives talk about "service management" as their new secret weapon. Intrigued, Albrecht researched this new focus and met with many of its early advancers, including Carlzon. Bolstered with Carlzon's message and convinced that he saw the parallels for American business, Albrecht went home with a new understanding of the true meaning of service quality as a competitive economic weapon.

Returning to the United States, Albrecht teamed up with fellow management writer Ron Zemke in 1985 to pen the best-selling "first look" at service management, *Service America!: Doing Business in the New Economy* (Dow Jones-Irwin). With the arrival of this book, service to the customer suddenly became a hot topic. Thanks to this book and the texts from Karl Albrecht and other thought leaders that followed, service quality changed from being *an* important factor in an organization's success to being *the* critical factor, the new agent for survival in our changing economy.

And now, nearly ten years hence, the service revolution continues to grow and grow.

> ➤ *But what about the TQM concept? Isn't that just as good as*
> *service management?*

If you compare the direction of the TQM, or Total Quality Management, movement with that of the service management revolution, you can see that they have followed parallel paths. But although their time frames and development histories are equivalent, little else matches. TQM is not service management, and service management—or TQS, Total Quality Service [1]—is not TQM. They are as dissimilar as carrots and ice cream, which are both foods, but look, feel, and taste different.

During its heyday in the late 1970s and its resurgence in the late 1980s, TQM worked wonders for some companies and failed miserably for others. On its face, TQM is like the Deming, Juran, and Crosby methods: It still measures outputs, by machines or by people. Nowhere in the original description of TQM is the word *customer*. And now that the concepts of service management, service quality, and customer value have such strong footholds in the business community, the TQM dilettantes are hurriedly trying to retrofit "the customer" into their old manufacturing-based model. It doesn't work that way.

TQM has never been about the customer. Trying to shove this square peg into a round hole defeats the real statistical, measurement, and quality-control uses of TQM and muddies the waters for true service management programs. It's easy to understand why so many businesspeople get confused.

Business book publishers still continue to crank out TQM books that have attempted to change TMQ historical connection with widget making. These authors try to sell us the idea that you can somehow shove the service employee and the customer into a model that was never designed for them in the first place. With all these initials and acronyms flying around, it's sometimes hard to separate the wheat from the chaff.

So here it is, warts and all: TQM is product-quality-focused and manufacturing-based; TQS is customer-focused and customer-based.

➤ *So what have we really learned in the past decade?*

In some ways, plenty. In others, surprisingly little. At least in some companies, large and small, the same mistakes in service management (or the lack thereof) keep getting made, over and over and over.

But since it's always easier to harp on the bad and never mention the good, let's take a quick look at two service success stories. While these two firms hardly classify as small businesses, I include them for two reasons:

- They are recognized for their commitment to the needs of the customer.

- More importantly, they look like fun places to work.

They are Disneyland and Federal Express (which, to include an important piece of trivia, FedEx CEO Fred Smith began with a loan from the Small Business Administration). Both are long-time members in the "Service Excellence Examples" club.

Disneyland is known all over the world for its ability to transport people (if only for a day) into a world of fun and fantasy. I'm sure that if you went to the jungles of the Congo or the snows of Antarctica, you could hold up a picture of Walt's famous mouse and someone in the crowd would shout, "Hey, there's Mickey!"

As many Disneyland watchers and service writers have recounted, park employees are referred to as "Cast Members" and there is a real commitment to the idea that says, "If you work here, you're 'on stage.' Everything you do when you're walking around or working out in our theme park is noticed by our guests and reflects upon Disneyland. We want people to enjoy our park as a total 'show business fantasy' experience. We try to whisk them away to a world that's fun and exciting. You participate in that fun and excitement process each time you interact with them in any way."

It may sound a bit corny to the hard-bitten types, but it works, and it works well.

I enjoy writing about Federal Express because I can honestly say that I have never had a disappointing service experience with them, ever. Not over the phone, not at the counter of their mail drop centers, and not with a driver picking up or delivering my packages. In our turbulent service society, that's darn rare, and I'd say even commendable. The people are always courteous and helpful, and even though I'm sure their job is demanding and filled with time pressures, they always figure out a way to add value to my service experience with them.

A Day at Disneyland

This story was recounted to me by a friend who is a noted national speaker. She uses this true tale as a way to commend Disneyland on its service attitude and to point out that no matter how expensive, difficult, time-consuming, or tedious something may turn out to be, sometimes you have to go the extra mile for the customer just because it's the right thing to do.

It seems that a woman and her four children were spending the afternoon on Tom Sawyer Island. If you recall the Disneyland design, this place is a small wooded island out in the middle of a man-made lake. You can climb trees, look at Indian camps and forts, and play with lots of other swell outdoors stuff.

When the woman rounded up her kids for the flat-bottomed boat trip back to the main part of Disneyland, she realized she was missing one child. Frantically, she searched several parts of the island, all to no avail. She enlisted the help of several Disneyland employees, who helped her scour the area from tip to tip. Still no child. Fearing the worst, the Disneyland people started a massive search party for the lost boy.

After several hours, fearing he might have drowned, they decided to bring in a scuba-diving team to search the area of the lake and look for the boy's body. The dive team suited up and went into the water.

It was at this exact moment that the woman suddenly looked up, slapped her forehead in amazement, and remembered that she had actually left the small boy back at home with her husband.

With shades of the movie *Home Alone* in their minds, the Disney staffers regrouped, cheerfully (and this is the true part) thanked the woman for remembering that her little son was safe, and went back to work.

Say what you want about her, it's still a great service story.

A Day at Federal Express

While this story lacks the drama of the Disneyland near-rescue event, it illustrates a commitment to the customer that is an all-too-rare event with other firms.

Our office had called the folks at FedEx to schedule a package pickup one Friday afternoon. FedEx promised to send a courier by the end of the day. By quitting time, no courier had arrived, and we became concerned. Sure enough, we missed the deadline, so we called to ask what had happened. Apparently, the communications people had misdirected the package person, and he had missed our stop. When we asked what we should do, the FedEx supervisor came on the line and told us, "Don't worry. We'll take care of this. Your package will be there on Monday as planned."

Early Saturday morning we were working in our offices when a route supervisor from Federal Express showed up, in street clothes and clearly on his day off. He picked up our package, profusely apologized for the delay, and promised to drive it down to the San Diego airport himself so that it would get out on the next eastbound plane. He did, and it did. Monday morning came, and right at 10:30 a.m., the package hit our client's desk in New York. Is this service above and beyond the call of duty? Absolutely.

Think of the last time you dropped your car off for repairs at a big car dealership and the mechanic told you, "I'll have her ready to go by 5:00." When you returned at 5:15 to pick it up, you heard, "The parts didn't come in, so the mechanic went home, and sorry, but we don't work weekends, so you'll just have to come back on

Monday to pick your car up." "Oh no, we don't offer free loaners or even rental cars here. That shop across the street offers those services, but not us."

You don't have to be huge to be good. You can add value to lots of your customers' experiences just through the little things you do for them. You can add value to your customer relationships in a variety of unique ways. There are things you and your front-line service providers can do for the customer that cost you little or nothing, but may be very valuable, important, or even charming for him or her.

FACTORS IN PERSONAL SERVICE

▶ *That sounds like you're saying we can even compete with our bigger competitors for the customer's business. What makes that possible?*

This question spins another: "Why do people even do business with small companies? Why don't they just go straight to the big guys to get what they need?"

Answer this for yourself. Do you patronize small businesses because you feel sorry for them and want to help them out? No. Is it because the "big guys'" stores, offices, plants, restaurants, and factories are too far away? No, again. Is it because they offer lower prices, more selection, or better value for your dollars? Not usually, since the chain stores, large factories, and other brand-name establishments buy in volume and thus can compete quite well on price and inventory. So what is it then? What makes you and the rest of the customers out there work with small businesses to meet your personal and professional needs?

If you guessed "personal service," you get a gold star. People often get a stronger sense of higher perceived customer value when they deal with small businesses. Consider the following factors that can help to make you as equally competitive as the big guys—not in every respect, but enough to generate the revenue, income, and market potential to help you thrive.

- *The "personal touch."* There is a lot to be said for this. A small mail-order catalog firm I do a lot of business with instantly pulls up my account on the computer when I call and mention my name. The telephone order person greets me warmly, asks if I'll be paying with the credit card they have on file for me, and generally makes me feel like we've been friends for years. The whole order-taking process is brief, painless, and comfortable.

  I have a favorite West Coast hotel where I stay often, even if I have to drive a bit farther into the city where I do business. I stay there enough to be on a nodding basis with the front desk staff. They always wave a greeting as I come and go over the span of a few days, even if they're busy with other guests. In some small way, this always makes me feel like a big shot, as if they're saying to the newly arriving customers in a nonverbal way, "That's Mr. Albrecht. He stays here frequently and is one of our best guests." I know that's not entirely true, but it always makes me feel well-heeled anyway.

  Because they recognize me as a person, not just a room number or a walking credit-card slip, I simply get more perceived value from my stays there.

  You surely have customers who you treat this way and I'm also sure you do business with companies on a personal and professional level that always make you feel like you're important. It's often the small things that matter the most.

- *Key employees who know them.* One of the standard scenes in the long-running syndicated tavern-based TV sitcom *Cheers* never fails to warm my service-minded heart. It occurs each and every time Norm (played by actor George Wendt) enters the bar and heads for his customary stool. In unison, bar patrons and bar employees shout out his name as he walks to his favorite spot for a beer and a sit. It makes me smile as I consider the power of this simple gesture in the real world.

This is not to say that you and your people have to be on a first-name basis with every single customer; that's not feasible, practical, or even attainable in most cases. But there is a lot to be said for doing business in a place where, to quote the *Cheers* theme song, "Everybody knows your name."

One of the reasons people get to be called regular customers is because they return. How you treat them is what makes them come back, tell their friends and associates, and continue to work with you for years.

- *Better product knowledge.* One of the things that plagues the big guys in certain industries and markets is higher-than-average employee turnover. It puts a definite damper on knowledge of the company's products when new members of the workforce must be constantly trained.

  Many small businesses have some dedicated long-time employees who know a tremendous amount about the products and services they sell, including which ones will work best for their customers and why.

- *More responsiveness to the often intangible critical factors that are important to the customer's report card.*

  Just as it's easy to get lost in the shuffle when you deal with large firms, it's easy for some things that are important to the customer to get missed or dismissed.

  This includes such unmeasurable service help like recommending other products or services to the customer based upon an identification of his or her wants and needs; adding a personal note, gift, insight, suggestion, or thought with the order; helping customers find what they want and staying around to answer questions; returning phone calls and letters promptly; solving small problems before they become big; and otherwise acting more like the customer's advocate or change agent and less like an employee who just wants to punch the clock, get the customer off his or her hands, and go home.

- *More responsiveness to tangibles like product quality, shipping deadlines, delivery dates, price concerns, etc.* Here again, many of these more objective issues—things that can be measured, analyzed, recorded, and followed through—slip through the cracks at a big corporation, leaving the customers feeling as if no one really wants to see them through the process of being a customer.

  Large and small companies do these tangible things well. If they are important to the customer, they should be important to you. So if you're sharp, you'll have an edge over the company that lets the little things go by unnoticed.

  This may mean making a checklist to see if all of the bases have been covered, asking other front-line service people, managers, or supervisors to "check off" on final work; or doing something as simple as asking the customer, "Is there anything else you need? Are there any questions about your product order or request for service that I can answer? Do you need to speak to anyone else? Is there any information you think I should have to help you now or later?"

- The potential for superior and longer relationships. Adding all these other issues up, the customer gets more of an overall feeling of closeness with the people he or she is doing business with. This just makes for better, longer, and more fulfilling relationships.

In nearly every sense, we all have choices, and we can make often compelling decisions about where we do business. Unless the above factors are a major part of the way you operate your small business, even if it's just in your own department, division, store, or small part of the factory you run, you can't capture the hearts, minds, and wallets of the customer.

As I'll illustrate and explain in later chapters, you don't necessarily have to be in charge to make important changes in the way you run your part of the world. When you're good, it helps others to be good.

All of this should show you what can you can do to compete and what can and should go right in top-quality service firms, but fear not, I haven't forgotten to mention some of the downsides. What follows are two examples of service quality programs run amuck, when management seeks to blame the employees for bad service report cards or when they fail to stoke the coals of a new service quality program.

Show Us Some Teeth: The Smile-Training Fiasco

In some organizations, the thinking appears to curve along these lines: "If there's something wrong with the way we serve our customers, it must be because of our employees. It's their fault. They need more training in how to be nice."

This usually leads to some type of seminar-based disaster known as "smile training," in which perfectly normal, functional, and grown-up adults get taught the rudimentary basics of simple courtesy, human decency, and the "proper behavior" to use in front of the customer. Here, a bright-eyed motivational speaker, image consultant, or self-appointed customer service expert comes into the company and sets about teaching the great mass of front-line service employees the art of being pleasant.

Guess what? It doesn't work because it attempts to fix the wrong problems. It also causes more harm than you'll ever know. In fact, the term *smile training* was created by the very same employees who were sent to these programs. If you get the distinct impression that the phrase has a negative connotation to many service people and is used derogatively as they trudge from one alleged customer service program to the next, you're right.

Here's a point to ponder if you're considering bringing in an expert to teach your people how to walk, talk, dress, and "display a winning attitude" around the customer: The problem in some organizations in which service is faulty is not always with the front-line people but with their *management*.

As a manager, supervisor, or executive, it is your job to help the front-line service providers by creating user-friendly systems that help them to do their jobs to the best of their ability. Let's take it for granted that you or your personnel people have hired adult workers with average or better-than-average social skills to work with your customers. If that's so, don't demean them by sending them to a training class that starts with the supposition that they need help with their manners.

Ask front-line service workers who have been through even one smile training seminar and they will tell you the following:

- We *don't* need to be told to use the customer's first or last name at least four times during each conversation. (Most customers don't like it any more than the employees do.)

- We *don't* need "helpful" slogans, patches, buttons, stickers, wall plaques, key chains, or paperweights to remind us to be nice to the customer. (We know what to say and do to be helpful, nice, and polite. Give us the means—through good systems, policies, and procedures—to help the customer by becoming his or her agent for success.)

- We *don't* need to be taught when to smile, when to say "Thank you," and when to say "Have a nice day." (The days of the happy-face button are long gone. We're not robots, we're human beings who have good days and bad, just like the people we serve. We know what it's like to be polite, and we know from our own experiences what kinds of treatment we like and don't like when we're the customer too.)

- We *do* need to be able to sit down with our managers and supervisors on a regular basis and talk about the ways we can work smarter and better, not necessarily faster, livelier, or like people who must pander to the customers' every whim. Allow us to have input into what goes on around here. We're on the line with the customer every day. We know what works and what doesn't, and we're brimming with several good ideas for improving that relationship.

- If you want to give us training, *do* make it adult-based, time-intensive, and of an added-value nature. Train us in the things that will ease our workload a bit, smooth rough edges in our customer interactions, or otherwise make us feel like valuable and necessary members of this organization.

Some of these smile-training episodes come about for entirely the wrong reasons. A rise in customer problems or complaints may indeed indicate a problem with one or more of your employees; these things happen, and a few bad apples get into the barrel. More likely, though, the complaints arise from *systems* problems that either hogtie the front-line service provider from being able to do a good job or force the customer to weave his or her way through your company's ill-conceived policies.

If you have one or five or twenty five bad employees—that is, employees who are not right for the job of serving the customer— then counsel them to change their methods and work habits, change their jobs or switch them to an internal position, or terminate them if you feel there is no hope and you have the legal grounds.

But if you're convinced that you have good employees for the most part, then it's time to take a look at *how* they do things rather than *what* they do with the customer.

If you have a terminally rude receptionist answering customer calls for you eight hours a day and this generates any number of mild or volatile complaints from those customers, then part of the blame must shift to you if you do nothing to replace, fire, transfer that employee, or switch him or her with someone more suited for the position.

But if your customer complaints all start to sound the same—

lost orders, missed deadlines, poor products, haphazard follow-ups, mangled communications, or other signs and symptoms of *systems* problems—you need to look past the employees, who may be valiantly trying to keep things running, all the while trying to catch your ear to tell you what needs repair.

Ask yourself this question as you look at your firm: "Are we doing the wrong things correctly or the right things incorrectly?" The answer may lie in your methods, not in your people.

FIZZLE FACTORS

In his book *The Only Thing That Matters*, Karl Albrecht offers a list of what he calls "Fizzle Factors," or reasons why most service programs go off the Cliffs of Mediocrity and into the Great Sea of Flops. If it seems to you that this list is painfully long, it's only because—as with many things in life and business—there are more ways to mess things up than to do them right.

At the risk of alienating or insulting the "big guys," I'll avoid any direct mention of their specific flops. Suffice to say you probably can describe some of the more notable ones you know from your industry or from what you read or hear in the business press. I realize that business newspaper and magazine articles can be amazingly critical of companies that try to change the way they serve their customers, but in many cases, sometimes the awful results speak for themselves.

On that happy note, here's a list of reasons why many service quality/customer value programs start out fine but end up going wrong:

Executive apathy

Here, the big chiefs give the go-ahead, assign the program to one or more of the Indians, and then go back to their respective top-level wigwams in a cloud of dust. They close the tent flap doors and move on to other "more important" matters. With no support from the top, no positive messages given from on high to the front-line service workers and their managers and supervisors, people start to get the feeling that nobody upstairs supports, defends, or cares about this new program.

They're usually right. If you don't have at least one senior executive on board who will tell everyone who asks, "I believe in this program and I'm going to give you my resources, time, money, and effort to make it work," you might as well just pack it in.

Service quality programs that succeed despite management indifference usually do so because a dynamic leader has come out of the lower management ranks to take charge, get results, and continue to guide and motivate the process. In some cases this person—if you're not already in the driver's seat—will have to be you.

Splintered executive commitment

This fizzle factor is almost as bad as apathetic leaders. Here, the house is divided. Some executives are committed to the principles of service management and want to move ahead with a wall-to-wall implementation that includes employee training, new strategies, new systems, and new ways to look at the needs and expectations of the customers.

Others aren't for this at all and have voted thumbs down. And still others are on what pollsters call the "mugrump" fence—that is, their mugs are hanging over one side and their rumps are hanging over the other. They may not want to commit themselves verbally or on paper if the rest of the top brass is not 100 percent behind the program as well.

Since support is sketchy—strong from some quarters and weak from others—the troops below get mixed messages. "Are they for this thing or not?", which leads to the natural follow-up question: "Well, if upper management's not going to support this new move, then why should we?"

Putting the wrong person in charge of a task force or quality initiative

This may be a leader or manager who is unskilled in the ways and means of the customer, has no ability to supervise and manage the front-line service providers and the related support staff, or is plainly just not the right man or woman for the job because of a host of behavioral or managerial factors.

This person may secretly (or even not so secretly) want to sabotage the program, make others look bad, or hog the limelight and the glory at the expense of others, or may just not have the education, people skills, or business savvy to run what should be a major, committed program for any firm.

And small businesses, with their often limited resources and assets, *really* can't afford to put this kind of boob behind the wheel.

Bureaucratizing the effort

Once the plans for any kind of new service quality program are in place, the red tape, the ad hoc committees, and the rulemongers appear. This fizzle factor is just as bad as executive apathy, only in reverse.

Here, the people at the top won't keep their collective mitts out of the soup. As a result, the front-line managers and service people may feel that they're being held back, reined in, or otherwise given a mixed message. "Are we going to do this thing now, or are we going to have another round of countless and endless meetings to talk about every detail?"

Sometimes the best way to start the program is to preach it, train it, and deliver it, then go ahead, turn 'em loose already.

Letting the program become a political football in the organization

Remember my discussion in Chapter 1 about "internal" and "external" customers. In this case, the internal customers have broken ranks and formed insidious groups or teams. They're now bent on using any new training program or service quality implementation plan as a bargaining chip, hostage, or sacred cow.

This commonly occurs between management ranks when no one feels that anyone is really in charge of the new change process.

Allowing the "I don't want to play" syndrome

Here, the department head or other similar manager decides to pick up his or her toys and go home. This can occur if he or she does not feel attached to the program, was not made part of the decision-making team, or otherwise feels put upon, left out, or mistreated in some real or imagined way.

If this person runs a unit, department, or division that is large enough, he or she can feed negative news to the people below all day long—not a good way to start any new program.

Allowing methodology battles among factions

In some organizations with a strong training contingent, certain pet theories, methodologies, and ways to get the program done will take center stage. These may compete with other favorite trainers, consultants, or inside and outside role players who may want their own input into or control over the new program.

Someone at the top needs to step in and say, "Listen, folks, I have chosen *this* method, *these* people to train it, and *these* people to implement it. Let's get back to work, shall we?"

Trivializing the objective

Smile training has reared its fat ugly head once more. Here, the presence of catchy slogans, buttons, and ad campaigns are used to try to convince everyone—employees and customers both—that something snappy is going to happen next. In reality, a little paint will be tossed around, and then it will be back to business as usual. Nothing ventured, nothing gained—certainly not more customers.

A client from a small bank approached one of my service management colleagues. "We need customer service training," he said, "and right away." When asked who this training was for, the banker replied, "For the tellers, of course. They need to know how to handle our customers better. We've been getting some complaints."

After asking some careful questions, my colleague got right to the point: "We don't do smile training for people who probably don't need it in the first place. It sounds as if you have a systems problem in your bank. Let's look at the ways your tellers have to do their jobs to meet the needs and expectations of the customer, then we'll look at training them to react to what they discover."

After a long pause on the other end of the phone, the banker said, "Thanks, we'll get back to you." You can guess the rest. Another band of innocent bank tellers was dragged off to a seminar on banking politeness.

Jumping off too soon without a clear sense of timing, sequence, and momentum

Good planning is the key to good decision-making. Any new service quality implementation will require plenty of work by advance teams. No matter what the size of the business, the senior managers and executives will have to roll up their sleeves, send out for coffee and sandwiches, and start making plans and decisions and doling out the necessary responsibilities to get people familiar with the service management concepts, into appropriate training for their jobs, and back out in front of the customer.

Rushing into anything causes mistakes and can lead the front-line employees to say, "Not again. Here we go on another wild goose chase while they try to figure out what they should do first or next."

Enthusiasm is great, but enthusiasm that is not backed by a clear plan and direction is useless. Even the most committed company leader can get only so far on adrenaline.

Contradicting the whole meaning of the effort with opposing messages

This is like pulling the plug on the bathtub drain before it's filled. This happens when companies and their leaders say they're committed to a service program, then turn right around and reassess; transfer or terminate key people; cut the training and development budget to the bone; or suddenly terminate the program until the market, the economy, or the next presidential administration improves.

Mixed messages kill good programs before they have a chance to work. These "both sides of our mouths" communications do little to offer any positive hope to the employees and the middle management who may actually be behind the ideas in the first place.

Axing the whole thing the first time the organization runs into rough sailing[2]

This is the "let's do this again next year" problem taken to an extreme. Or, if various factions or unhappy groups give some initial resistance, senior management decides not to press the issue and backs down. Worse yet, if the number of customer criticisms or complaints actually rises for a period (not uncommon as new programs get underway), management is quick to revert back to type.

A careful review of these dull moments in the young life of a service quality program points to one key factor: The need for high-level enthusiasm from the owners or operators of the company. Positive commitment to any new service program by senior management is essential for its success.

Notes

1. "TQS" or "Total Quality Service" is a registered trademark of The TQS Group, 180 N. LaSalle, Ste. 1101, Chicago, IL 60601, (312) 201-1411.

2. Karl Albrecht, *The Only Thing That Matters: Bringing the Power of the Customer to the Center of Your Business*, (New York: HarperCollins, 1992) 206-207.

Chapter 3

The Service Triangle: Centering on the Customer

"The customer is never wrong."
—In R. NEVILL and C. E JERNINGHAM'S
"Piccadilly to Pall Mall" (1908)

TRUE CUSTOMER FOCUS, OR HOW TO HOLD ON TO YOUR CUSTOMERS WITH A ROPE, NOT A SLOGAN

If you take but one solitary piece of advice from this book about how to start turning your organization toward the customer, it should be this: Make real changes in the way you care for the customer's needs; don't just invest in slogans and hope that a few words will make a big difference with either your customers or your people.

Even if you stopped reading this book at this point, that counsel alone would be enough to steer you in the right direction. It's not enough just to talk about making improvements and changes in the way the customer is treated. It's more a philosophy, a driving principle, or an operating plan that starts at the top and trickles down to every level in the organization.

Revving up the workers with some lapel pins, buttons, hats, ribbons, and bumper stickers works for about a week. The real effect comes when all the people in the company align themselves in the same direction. It's not posters in the employee breakroom that change things, it's leadership based on research, commitment, and the ability to identify who needs what—employees and customers—and giving it to them.

Preach One Message and One Message Only

There's an old saying in advertising that applies to life as well: "If something works, stick to it." In the early part of his presidency, John F. Kennedy made a simple, declarative statement that became one of the most significant driving forces for our nation at that time. He said, "We will put a man on the moon by the end of the decade." On July 20, 1969, Kennedy was posthumously proven correct in his assertion. We did it.

Putting Neil Armstrong's first footprints on the lunar surface called for a tremendous influx of cash into the coffers of NASA and its partners. Scientists, ground crews, astronauts, and builders, designers, and engineers of every stripe poured their hearts, minds, and bodies into the task.

The value of Kennedy's request was not only that it put a man on the moon; that was merely the result. The importance of his words was what they did to our country. The Russians had already shown us their intention to beat us in the space race. Kennedy saw the need to mobilize the country behind a single theme: a lunar landing by an American, and done in less than ten years.

Sad to say, we have not seen such fervor since then. We've been excited about a lot of things, but that one moment in our recent history seemed to serve as a catalyst for a nation.

Perhaps another example was spoken by then-President George Bush during the early rumblings of the Iraqi Gulf War. Bush took to the airwaves and said something that appeared here on posters, on signs, and on the helmets of American soldiers everywhere: Free Kuwait.

Those two words energized us at home and abroad as few others have. Witness the massive parades for our victorious troops and the fact that previously well-insulated Army generals Colin Powell and Norman Schwarzkopf were given cultlike hero status after they directed the drive that sent Saddam Hussein's soldiers fleeing from Kuwait City.

Not surprisingly, most of the other nonpolitical one-idea messages we remember come from advertising. Even if your favorite is not on this list, you can certainly remember a dozen more just like these:

Coke is it

(If you removed the brand name from this phrase and showed it to 1,000 fourth-graders, I'd bet nearly all of them would come up with the product in no time flat.)

Bayer works wonders

(A journalism professor at the University of Missouri— Columbia School of Journalism said that these three short words tell a powerful story about this product. "It just wouldn't work in the passive voice," he told his students. "'Wonders are worked by Bayer' just doesn't have the same impact.")

Federal Express—When it positively, absolutely has to be there overnight

(Is there any doubt about when the package will arrive?)

Snapple—Made from the best stuff on earth

(True or not, it's a great, simple statement about a pure, simple product).

My point comes back to focus, unity of purpose, and direction. Companies that try to come up with a universal theme or a driving message that is too broad in scope can fragment their total efforts. "Put a man on the moon" is easy to get behind; a 200-page diatribe about space exploration is not. And so it goes with companies—especially small ones, which have less time or money to waste on organizing the troops.

And the only thing worse than a message that is too long, too all-encompassing, or too detailed is one that is too trivial. The problem with the trivial platitudes that often headline new service programs is that they can't be personified, engaged, or put into immediate use by a group of reasonably intelligent folks, otherwise known as your employees.

An irritating and exasperatingly familiar example comes to mind: the ever-popular and increasingly ridiculed "The customer is always right." You've seen the related "inspirational" posters that say, "This is Rule 1. Rule 2 is, when in doubt, see Rule 1."

What's so wrong with "The customer is always right"? For one thing, you can't get the average teenage kid who works in a fast-food restaurant, gas station, or grocery store to believe it, and it doesn't sell very well to the average adult front-line service provider either. Why? Because sometimes the customer is wrong.

Try as we may, we can't meet every single customer's needs every single time. As members of the human race, we all make mistakes, and customers are no different. They are not always right, just as we are not always right.

This doesn't mean you can't become the customer's advocate or his or her change agent. Why not say this?

The customer's problem should become our problem.

What's the difference? Plenty. "The customer is always right" is neither very true nor very motivating. It doesn't tell your front-line people what to *do* about or for the customer.

And yet, some companies still can't let go of this old platitude that, for them, epitomizes the real meaning of service. Some businesspeople's idea of a *service strategy* is to have it embossed every nonliving thing in their office, factory, or store. Even after all this time, they still feel that their people should live and die by this hackneyed credo.

The problem with this service strategy is that it's actually a service bumper sticker, not an operating principle for the whole company. Demanding that your employees eat, sleep, and live by it can put them into awkward positions. Let's face it, sometimes the customer is dead wrong, and sometimes there is little you or anyone who works for you can do to change that fact.

There is a well-known service story that comes from the Nordstrom department store chain. This firm is famous for its utter devotion to its customers, and any time you're that committed to the customer, good and interesting stories are bound to come out.

It seems that on one fateful day, an elderly woman came into her local Nordstrom's and demanded that she be given a refund for a tire she had purchased at the store. (Freeze frame for a second: Nordstrom does not, has not, and will not sell tires in its stores, yesterday, today, or tomorrow. Now back to our story.)

The salespeople politely tried to explain to the woman that they did not sell such an item and that she must be mistaken. "Oh no," came the old woman's reply. "I know I bought this here, and you're supposed to give me my money back whenever I'm not satisfied with your products. I'd like a refund."

After some careful discussion among the employees, and some careful thought by a supervisor, the good folks at Nordstrom took back "their" tire and cheerfully gave the woman a complete cash refund for it. She left fully satisfied and returned to shop, shop, shop another day.

Now, the fact that the woman, albeit old and perhaps a wee bit daft, was a long-time Nordstrom shopper with the charge slips to prove it may have had more than a little to do with the refund for said tire. Further, the motto at Nordstrom is "Do what it takes to care for the customer." The employees are given great latitude to help the company keep its well-deserved reputation as a truly customer-focused retailer.

What's the point of this heart-warming tire tale? The customer was wrong, plain and simple. The good folks at Nordstrom adjusted to her error and corrected the problem in a novel way, but she was still wrong. Saying "the customer is always right" is in some case ludicrous, in others naive, and in others, financially threatening for your company.

➤ *Okay, I get your point. So if the customer's not always right, what do I tell my service people?*

This doesn't mean you can't become the customer's agent or his or her service advocate. Maybe a better way to rephrase the above-mentioned golden oldie is:

We meet our customers' needs, maximize their expectations, and solve their problems.

Isn't this a better way of expressing what "The customer is always right" (T.C.I.A.R.) so haphazardly says? In this statement, you put yourself, your company, and your employees into the position of meeting needs and offering solutions. This also helps to lessen or prevent impossible situations (like Nordstrom tire sales) that put your front-line service providers into expensive, embarrassing, or argumentative positions with difficult customers.

That's the other vexing part of the T.C.I.A.R way of doing business: It doesn't take into consideration the fact that on rare occasions, we work with irate, obnoxious, or tiresome customers. They are not always right, and in some extreme cases we may not even want to do business with them.

But by focusing our efforts on meeting needs and expectations and solving problems, we can deal with even the most difficult customers in a more balanced manner.

THE SERVICE TRIANGLE: A FRAME OF REFERENCE WE CAN ALL UNDERSTAND

If you haven't quite bought into the idea of the customer-powered business, here's a new frame of reference that may help you clarify what's going on around you.

The remainder of this chapter is based upon Karl Albrecht's "service triangle™," a customer-centered model he created to emphasize the role of service systems, service strategies, and service people in any successful organizational program.

In short order, you'll know what the triangle is, how it works, and, more importantly, how you can define and clarify it to meet your own small-business needs.

Fig. 3.1
The Service Triangle [1]

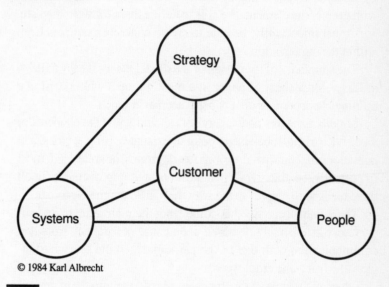

© 1984 Karl Albrecht

Looking at Figure 3.1, you can see that while it's simple in design, it's powerful in application. Each of the four parts are interlocked and interrelated. You can't have one without the others, and each of the outer elements—the service strategy, the service systems, and the service people—work together and separately to revolve around the most important member of the service triangle—the customer.

➤ *Is this model for every business? Who should understand it as a part of his or her job in my company?*

The service triangle was designed for all businesses. It focuses on the most important elements for success with your customers. You'll need all of them in place to begin your movement toward capturing more market share, beating your competitors in a variety of added value areas, and becoming a customer-powered business.

As far as who needs to know about the service triangle, that largely depends upon the roles of the people in your organization. Certainly everyone at the top management level should be familiar with each of the elements, be able to define them for what they are, and, most importantly, be able to create concrete examples from within the organization.

The simplicity of the design of the model makes it easy to draw quickly—on a sheet of paper in a meeting, on a whiteboard in a training classroom, or on a paper placemat at lunch.

Middle managers and supervisors should know the elements of the service triangle; be able to point to examples, people, cases, and operations in their own divisions, work groups, or areas; and, most importantly, be able to offer suggestions and improvements in all three areas with respect to the way they surround the customer.

These enhancements that come from the management and supervisory level should be based upon constant feedback from and communication with one of the participants in the service triangle—the front-line employees.

Often, the people in the trenches, who do the important day-to-day work that keeps them in contact with either the customers or other employees who actually serve the customers, can be your best source of information. They know what works and what doesn't, in terms of your systems. They may be able to provide helpful feedback in your creation of an overall service strategy, and they certainly know how their fellow service workers handle the customers.

And even though they may not always be involved in the major strategy decisions that affect the company, the front-line people should know of the service triangle and what it means to them and to the organization. You should always encourage service quality-related suggestions (and other good ideas as well) from the folks who do the real work with the people you're most interested in—the customers.

With that in mind, let's get to the discussion of the elements in the service triangle:

The Top Position—The Service Strategy

It's not enough that *you* know your company's service strategy; your customer has to know about it as well. Why? For one thing, customers want to know what they can expect from a company when they do business with it.

And it's not enough to say that you give good service or that your product is better than your competitors'; you have to demonstrate this fact, and you can do it by creating a service strategy that tells one and all, "This is what we are all about. This is *why* we are in business. Here is what we do for you."

The creation of this strategy requires careful thought and a hard look at what business you're in. You've got to look at yourself in a different light, the way the customer does.

Here's an easy example: If you own a paint store, you're *not* just in the paint business. When your customers come in, they aren't just looking for paint. They want paint that will match their decors, improve the look of their homes, make their spouses happy, resist dirt and scuffs, go up and on in one coat, and last for a long time.

You are not just a paint provider; you're a paint problem-solver, a paint advice-giver, and a paint representative for your customers. All of your paint store employees should feel this way as well.

The Left Position—The Service Systems

What's the new injury-of-the-month in today's hectic offices, stores, and factories? The dreaded carpal tunnel syndrome, which affects the inner and outer muscles and tendons of the wrists, and afflicts this nation's computer users, typists, telephone operators, radio dispatchers, desktop publishing designers, grocery store checkers, cashiers, butchers, bakers, and candlestick makers.

This injury, which can cause mind-numbing pain to the wrists and hands of those it strikes, is caused by repetitive motion movements. In theory, any wrist-oriented, limited-range-of-movement activity that you do over and over and over could make you susceptible to carpal tunnel abuse.

With millions in insurance, medical, disability, and retirement settlement dollars going out because of this problem, the companies and people who paid these bucks decided to look at the cause of this injury and see if they could stop it. They chose two paths of inquiry: Can we change the *way* we *do* things, and can we change what we *use* to do them?

Now the office supply catalogs are full of ergonomically correct devices designed specifically to avoid carpal tunnel syndrome. Special split-level computer keyboards, padded "mouse" handrests for weary Macintosh or Windows users, wrist braces, hand pads, and a variety of chairs, tables, and other equipment have been introduced to combat this expensive affliction.

And besides the devices, gizmos, and gear, the people who wanted to prevent these injuries looked at *how* people did their jobs, e.g., "Can we change the job of the computer operator to give him or her more breaks, additional duties away from the keyboard, or a different way to do the actual work?"

In short, they focused on how to change *systems* to make them less painful and more user-friendly. This, to make a short story long, is what you'll need to do in your organization to make it more *customer-friendly*.

A few points should be clear in your mind before you go about the organization changing the way people do things:

- *Look before you leap.* Changing the way people do their tasks is one thing; altering the shape, size, and direction of the firm is quite another. If something is not being done to your satisfaction, fix the problem, but don't barge in and change things just for the sake of churning up the organization.

- *Change at the front-line level, for the most part, should come as a result of employee consensus, not because of some high-and-mighty management edict.* Your employees want to know why things change, and they want to have some input, even if it's only a minute amount, into the discussion. Better yet, since they're the ones who do much of the work that may fall into the category of change for the benefit of the customer, they can serve as your best sounding board for new and better ideas.

- *Sometimes it's not systems or the way we do things that need changing, it's the people who need changing.* Putting your rudest employee at the front counter is not a cry for a systems change, it's a red flag for a personnel change. Hiring is never an easy process and with the glut of people out there who want service positions but lack the necessary "people" skills, you have the right to be very choosy about who you select.

- *Have a heart.* Most of us thrive on the routine, stability, and safety in our jobs. If we wanted to be sword swallowers, oil-well firefighters, parachutists, or deep-sea divers, we would have signed up for those jobs when the clipboard came around. Drastic, overly frequent, or mindless changes should be avoided because of the stress "spikes" they cause in your people. Nobody wants to come into work one morning and see his or her desk in another part of the building, or find that he or she has a whole new set of unexpected duties, or both. Humane people management is not a contradiction in terms.

The next chapter and, more specifically, Chapter 7, will help you look at your systems, analyze what needs to stay and what needs to go, and create good ways to do new things or better ways of doing old things.

The Right Position—The Service People

There's a clever way to help you remember why your service providers—those very important people who serve the customer—are seated in the right position: To succeed as a customer-driven organization, you need the "right" people in the "right" jobs, doing the "right" things at the "right" time.

You can have the best products, the best location, the prettiest colors, the cleanest rest rooms, the tastiest foods, the lowest prices, and on and on, and it won't mean anything if you've got the wrong people serving the customer. This element of the service triangle should lead you to ask:

As I look around the organization, are my best and brightest people heavily involved with serving our customers? Or did they move on to other jobs, leaving the Drudges, the Lazys, and the Don't-Cares in their wake? Is it time for me to evaluate each of our personnel for not only the tasks they perform, but for the way they interact with and treat the customer?

Some performance review sheets give this subject short shrift. Checking a few boxes marked "Excellent, Average, or Poor" is not the way to rate the level of quality care your customers receive from your employees. It's got to go deeper than that.

As you wander through your organization watching your service people interact with your customers, what is your overall feeling? Pleasure and confidence? Dread and dismay?

It may be paradoxical, but did you ever notice in your own personal service encounters, those powerful moments of truth that make up every part of a service experience, that sometimes the worst people tend to staff some of the highest-profile service positions in an organization?

Think back a bit for yourself. Have you gone to a coffee shop in search of a quick bite, only to find the surliest host or hostess ready to fling your menu at you as you sat at the table?

When you're in a hurry and need to rent a car, was the counterperson talking on the phone to someone while he or she processed your request?

Did your bank teller process your transaction with the usual "Thanks-Have-a-Nice-Day — Next!" mentality?

Maybe you've been extraordinarily lucky and these failed moments of truth have never happened to you. However, chances are that you can add dozens of other similar stories to this short list, especially if you travel frequently, do business with a variety of service-related companies, or like to keep a close eye on the activities of your competitors.

Most good service companies have learned that you get more customers with sweetness than with vinegar. And it's no accident that they've put their shining stars in most of the critical front-line customer-contact positions.

Sharp people *belong* "on the line" with the customer. They relish their interaction with their customers and thrive on the give-and-take contact the moments of truth bring to both sides.

The Center Position—The Customer

There's a good and obvious reason why the customer is in the center position in the service triangle. All of the other elements revolve around the customer. While none of them are as important as the customer, and the proper development and understanding of each alone is critical, they work best in harmony with one another.

In a perfect world, your customers would pile into your place of business like ants at a chocolate factory; buy out all your stock or use your services to full capacity; invite their friends, their colleagues, and even total strangers to enjoy the fruits of your business, pay top dollar happily; and come back again and again until you could afford to retire at a tender age.

In the real world, your customers need to be lured to your store, factory, or office like wily old bass in the big lake. You must tempt them with painfully competitive prices (and thin margins), and superior service, and beg them—either literally or through rewards, advertising, or other expensive means—for more business and referrals, then wake up and do it all over again the next day because they still might get a better offer next door and take it.

The elements of the service triangle suggest that you hope for the best, but you still have to work very hard anyway. You'll need to develop a plan that starts at the beginning and ends at the beginning again—in short, a never-ending keep-the-customer loop.

Here are the most important factors involving that very important part of your business: the customer.

Understand the customer

First, you do this by knowing what business you're in and why anyone should want to patronize that business.

Second, you get some data about your customers ranging from the demographic (age range, sex, salary level, discretionary income, distance from you to them, education, etc.) to the more abstract but necessary information (buying habits, price "flinch" levels, tastes, styles, willingness to be flexible, etc.).

Discover what the customer needs or wants

You do this by simply asking—either face to face, by telephone, by mail-in survey, by reply card, or by any other successful means you know of to get the customer to tell you what he or she likes or doesn't like about the products or services you offer.

Plan to change the color of your most popular item from green to blue? Better ask first. Plan to change your hours from "Open at 8:00 a.m." to "Open at 10:00 a.m."? Better run it by your customers, who may plan *their* day around *you* and would rather *you* think about planning *your* day around *them*.

Give the customer what he or she wants

Based on your review of solid data, verified feedback, and your understanding of your market and your competitors, you can start to meet customers' needs. If the majority of your customers say, "We want white bed sheets in the rooms," "more choices on the menu," "a better design of your sprinkler parts," "smaller or larger boxes," "longer hours at your drive-up tellers," "a choice of more colors in your curtain shop," or "french fries shaped like seahorses," you had better be ready to adapt and change to meet those needs.

The streets are full of ugly stories of companies—large and small—that failed to listen to what their customers wanted and drastically changed something, or that heard their customers ask for changes and failed to make these changes in time.

You probably know about other product disasters that were created from within the organization. Coca-Cola made the mistake of tinkering with its century-old soda formula, with near-disastrous results. Consumers hated the new Coke, screamed for the old one, and helped to leave a seemingly intelligent, well-run organization with egg on its face.

How many times have we seen companies try to reinvent the wheel and fix what was not broken? "Here's a new product we're sure you'll love as much as or more than the old one," they crow to their customers. And when that product "tanks" in the marketplace, they're left to scramble for their now-dwindling market share. "Come back!" they plead with departing customers as they lurch back in the original direction, desperately trying to find the magic formula, when perhaps they had it all along.

Serve the customer in as many ways as possible

This is a broad mission, but one that leads to many different possibilities, new sidelines, and expanded product and service lines.

One of the best ways to do this is by thinking creatively about your products or services and asking this question: "What do we sell now that could be bundled with another item?"

Some random examples: bookstores that sell coffee, tea, and sweets to their browsing customers; baby food companies that offer baby clothes; photo finishing companies that offer portrait services; hardware stores that offer installation; grocery stores that deliver; fitness centers that sell vitamins and nutrition supplements; pizza shops that offer videotape rentals; and so on.

I'm sure that if you thought hard enough, you could come up with a dozen different ways to add more value to the products and services you sell by putting different ones together. And remember that your front-line service people are one of the best sources for these kinds of innovative ideas.

Ask yourself, "What can we offer now to the customer that we haven't before, in terms of additional service?" And keep in mind that it's not just physical items that make a difference. Mints on hotel pillows, free valet parking at the restaurant, and car washes with an ten-gallon minimum gasoline purchase are great, but what about the "people" side?

The service management success story that is the Wal-Mart department store chain is not just based on low prices. That the company has taken the initiative to put a "greeter" at the front door of every store says something about the way it wants its customers to feel. It's people, not just low prices, that win hearts.

And Wal-Mart is not shy about publicizing the good deeds of its service people in its advertising campaigns. While other companies keep this information close to the chest or ignore it all together, Sam Walton's company gives it Page One status.

A customer from New Jersey writes to the Wal-Mart manager in Baton Rouge, Louisiana to sing the praises of a Wal-Mart sales associate:

> I recently bought a large dormitory refrigerator at your store. It was for my daughter, who was moving into a dorm at Louisiana State University. When we got to our car, we saw the refrigerator wouldn't fit. One of your sales associates noticed our predicament. Although he was on his way to lunch, he loaded the refrigerator in his truck, drove it to the motel where we were staying, and unloaded it. When I offered to pay him, he politely refused. He told us that as a Wal-Mart associate, service is just a part of his job. In today's world not many people go out of their way to help others. Needless to say, this young man made a big impression on us.[2]

When was the last time you or your company publicly celebrated the service accomplishments of one of your people? When was the last time you rewarded someone who went out of his or her way to do something good for the customer? Everybody likes praise, especially when they go the extra mile. A paycheck isn't enough; a public pat on the back, a free lunch, a reserved parking space, an extra coffee break, a half-day off, or even a photo in the company newsletter can pay huge dividends for you, the employee who receives the accolade, and the other people around him or her who see that hard work, good service skills, and concern for the customer are not only important here but worthy of reward.

Keep the customer coming back

Repeat business is one of the cornerstones of small-business success. It's no secret that the more you can get good, current customers to return, the better you'll do. So why is it that some businesses spend so much time and energy trying to get new customers rather than working harder to satisfy the current ones?

Books and books have been written about how it's more expensive to attract new customers than it is to keep current ones. If this is true, why not turn more of your efforts toward keeping high marks on the customer's report card?

Get referrals from the customer

Word of mouth is a great, inexpensive marketing tool. Whatever you can do to encourage your customers to advertise for you is money and time well spent. Offer rewards for good referrals, like coupons, free merchandise, discounted prices for services, bonus items, extensions on warranties, better service contracts, gifts, praise, and even public notoriety.

And don't just wait for the customer to bring his or her friends, family, or colleagues through the door; encourage your employees to do the same, and create reward systems for them as well. (As I'll discuss in Chapter 6, about employee empowerment, this is also a great way to get good new employees for your firm.)

Repeat the process forever

As leading management theorist Peter Drucker often warns, "Whom the gods wish to punish, they first grant forty years of business success." With many service programs, after early accomplishments there can be a plateau period in which things do not go as smoothly as they did in the beginning. As we've seen in the previous discussions about the fizzle factors, that's not the time to abandon the mission.

Instead, redouble your efforts by continuing to fine-tune the elements of the service triangle as they relate to one another and to the customer.

QUALITY SELF-SERVICE

➤ *My business involves an element of self-service. Sometimes my customers have to do things for themselves? Does the service triangle still apply?*

Yes, but in addition to what you've already learned about it, there are three other hard-and-fast rules here:

1. **Make sure your equipment is in perfect working condition.** Whether it's ATM machines; gas pumps; stamp machines; food; soda, or candy vending machines; paint mixers; tire fillers; mustard dispensers; ticket machines; car wash equipment; or whatever, everything the customer touches or sees must be in top working order.

    In reality, your self-service business is one big moment of truth. If there are no employees immediately on the spot to demonstrate your products or services to the customers or to help them use these things correctly, you'll have to rely on the customer to make the right choices. The moments of truth start when customers reach your premises and don't end until after they've left.

2. **Make sure the instructions on how to work your equipment are clear and easy for everyone to understand.**

Nothing is more maddening than not knowing how to work some piece of machinery. (Nothing frustrates a man more, except perhaps getting lost in the car and not wanting to ask for directions in front of his wife.) We've all been involved in service episodes where the instructions for whatever we needed to operate were missing, faded beyond reading, or written in such a way as to baffle even the manufacturer.

This again is a critical moment of truth: The customers can either figure it out and get what they need and want, or not. If they don't, they're probably not coming back, and you'll never even hear about it. Unless you get a complaint letter or an angry phone call, you could go on your merry way and never know there is a problem until it's too late to bring back those lost customers.

This again raises the issue of being able to take off your owner's or manager's hat and go back to thinking like a customer. If you can't work something exactly right the first time, chances are your customers can't either. You'll get failing grades on a report card you may never even see.

3. **Have someone available to help your customers if they cannot operate your equipment.** Even if there are no employees on-site and the best you can possibly do is have someone answer questions over the telephone, make it easy for your customers to get immediate help if necessary. We've all experienced episodes of complete frustration when the gas pump didn't work, the vending machine kept our money, or the teller machine ate our card.

Don't leave the customer hanging; make qualified help available—and this does not mean someone who is paid to take phone messages or tell the customer to wait until the maintenance guy gets back from lunch.

Your customer service people should be on-line in some high-tech fashion and ready to offer assistance, advice, and even a kind word to a customer who may feel dumb for even asking for help.

A Last Look at the Elements

So, to review the elements of the Service Triangle™ one final time, keep these driving factors in mind as you create and fill in the blanks for your company's own service triangle design. Put your creation on paper, and be prepared to talk about it with the people who can help you implement it, using whatever means you have at your disposal. Remember, you don't have to be in charge of everything to be able to take charge of something.

You can create a custom-made service triangle for your organization if it includes the following:

- **An effective service strategy.** This tells everyone in your organization what's expected of them, what the company will do for them and for the customer, and how the organization plans to deliver quality service. (I'll discuss this in great detail in Chapter 4.)

- **Customer-friendly systems in place.** These support the employees in everything they say and do—alone, together, and for the customer. All systems must be arranged to make it *easier,* not harder for your service providers to help the customer, or easier, not harder, for the customer to serve himself or herself.

- *Customer-powered front-line service providers.* This starts with good people, given good tools to do good things—well-supervised, well-managed employees who are still given enough leeway to become the customer's agent, take care of his or her needs, and maximize his or her expectations in a flexible, thorough, and even thoughtful manner.

Notes

1. The Service Triangle model, diagram, figure, and elements is a registered and protected trademark of Karl Albrecht, c/o Karl Albrecht & Associates, 4320 La Jolla Village Drive, Suite 310, San Diego, CA 92122-1204, (619) 622-4884.

2. Copyright 1994 advertising material from the Wal-Mart Corporation, Fayettesville, Arkansas.

Chapter 4

Understanding Your Customers: New Maps and New Meanings

"Business has only two basic functions—marketing and innovation."

—PETER DRUCKER

Many small-business owners don't have the faintest notion of what it's like to be a customer—especially of their own company—any more. Using the Cycle of Service, this chapter takes you through a handy review course which, if it were offered in business school, might be called "Customer Service 101: Seeing Your Company Through the Customer's Eyes."

You'll review the steps your typical customers take when they do business with your firm. And these steps should serve as your new frame of reference by showing you exactly the areas that need change.

The other significant reason for a step-by-step review of the customer's experience with your firm is that it also helps to make visible how your *employees* work around this experience with their customers. So besides being a measure of the customer's experience with your company, it also casts a sharp eye on your service systems. By seeing what the customer goes through to do business with you, you can see what might need an adjustment from a systems standpoint.

THE CYCLE OF SERVICE: HOW TO SEE THINGS FROM THE CUSTOMER'S POINT OF VIEW

Whenever you travel to a place you've never been, it's always best to bring a map. When customers come to your company, they are guided by their own "maps"—previous service experiences with your firm or ones like it, life experiences, service histories, and recommendations from others.

To put it in its simplest terms, in order to go where the customer goes, you need a special kind of map to help both of you get to your destination, a quality service experience. For help, let's look at a map known as the Cycle of Service.

This mapping process consists of three basic, but often unheeded parts:

- The beginning. This is the point at which the customer first comes into contact with you, your people, your systems, and some or all of your entire organization. If you guessed that this is also the doorway to the service concept known as the *moment of truth*, you are correct. At the start, the customer is making certain basic, intuitive, or even sophisticated value judgments about your company.

- The middle. As the service experience continues, more and more moments of truth are piling up in the customer's mind.

- And the end of the customer's experience. At this point, the customer has completed business with you, and his or her mental report card has already posted a grade. Some people use their own "pass/fail" system—Was this a good experience? Would I come here again? Others are more diligent: What went right here? What went wrong? What did I like? What did I not like?

As Figure 4.1 indicates, the Cycle of Service is a series of moments of truth your customer goes through as he or she experiences the service your organization delivers. Whereas you and your people might see these steps or increments along this circular cycle as tasks to complete, the customer sees each situation, taken singly and together, as a complete service experience.

The Cycle of Service is really a map of your company's systems, broken down into increments, steps, decisions, duties, and activities, all designed to take the customer from the front door, through the company, and back out the front door again. While the Cycle of Service says nothing about your hope that the customer will want to repeat the process with you again, this hope should be built into your thought processes.

Figure 4.1
Cycle of Service

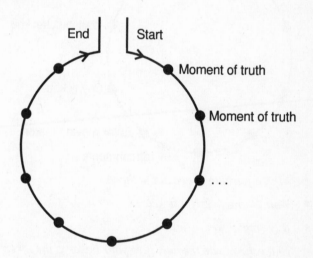

The power behind the Cycle of Service is the way it helps you see things that are unique from the customer's point of view. The more you can see, understand, and experience the same things as your customer, the better equipped you'll be to fix what needs fixing or adjust what's working well.

Let's choose a common service experience and map it out along the Cycle of Service. As you read and follow the progression, put yourself into that customer's shoes.

Here, you've decided to go to a movie. Figure 4.2 gives the Cycle of Service from beginning to end, starting when you leave your house and drive to the theater:

Figure 4.2
The Cycle of Service Goes to the Movies

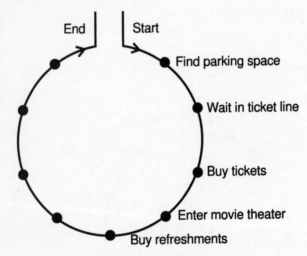

- *Find a parking space at the theater.*
- *Wait in line to buy a ticket.*
- *Buy your ticket.*
- *Enter the movie theater; give your ticket to the taker.*
- *Wait in line to buy popcorn and soda.*
- *Pay for your food.*
- *Go to the rest room before the movie.*
- *Go into the theater and find a seat.*

- *Sit and watch the movie.*
- *Leave the theater and go back to your car.*

These ten steps in Figure 4.2 represent a sample of your total customer experience at the movies. For clarity and length, I've left out many lesser details, but this trip to the theater represents a common experience for most of us. What you're experiencing, literally, is ten separate moments of truth.

You, as the customer, are constantly making conscious or subconscious value judgments about each of the moments of truth you encounter. These value judgments go onto that mental report card you carry in your head.

It's just like when you were in school; these events either exceed your expectations or needs, meet them, or fail to meet them. All customers give you these kinds of "grades" each time they do business with you. Just because you don't hear them out loud doesn't mean they're not being tallied.

Let's break them down and look at what could go right and what could go wrong during this excursion into movie-time service.

- *Find a parking space at the theater.*

    Exceeds Expectations: You find a nice, roomy space in a well-lighted area, close to the front door, and away from those people with their notorious door-denting cars. You see a security guard walking around the lot, keeping an eye on things.

    Meets Expectations: You find a space not too close and not too far away from the door.

    Fails Expectations: You do not find any parking space in the entire lot and have to park across the road from the theater building.

- *Wait in line to buy a ticket.*

  Exceeds Expectations: No line; no wait to get your ticket.

  Meets Expectations: A short line; not much wait for your ticket; still enough seats left inside for you.

  Fails Expectations: A long line and a long wait to get your ticket, or a long line and all tickets sold out for that showing.

- *Buy your ticket.*

  Exceeds Expectations: Low bargain prices that you didn't expect; a friendly ticket seller who makes pleasant conversation and tells you to enjoy the show; correct change from your bill and a coupon for a discount on your next ticket purchase.

  Meets Expectations: Standard prices; a polite ticket seller; correct change; no problems getting a ticket.

  Fails Expectations: Higher than expected prices; a rude, surly, or downright dishonest ticket taker who snaps at you, talks on the phone to his or her friends during the transaction, or shortchanges you $10 and declares that you're wrong.

- *Enter the movie theater; give your ticket to the taker.*

  Exceeds Expectations: A spotless lobby; a charming ticket taker who makes you feel glad you chose that particular movie, gives directions to the theater, and gives you a quick reminder about a new movie coming next week.

  Meets Expectations: A clean, well-kept, and well-lighted lobby, and a polite ticket taker who directs you to the correct theater.

  Fails Expectations: A filthy lobby with food and trash on the floor; a sour ticket taker who shoves your stub into your hand, says, "Next!" and motions for you to move along.

- *Wait in line to buy popcorn and soda.*

  Exceeds Expectations: No line, a courteous and friendly counterperson who explains the best popcorn and soda bargains for your money, and a cheery sendoff as you head for the cashier.

  Meets Expectations: A short line, a helpful counterperson, the right food you ordered, a polite thank you.

  Fails Expectations: A long, disorganized line full of angry patrons; a rude counterperson who gives you the wrong food and tries to hustle you through his or her station like it was an auto plant assembly line.

- *Pay for your food.*

  Exceeds Expectations: Lower than average prices, the correct change, and a cheerful cashier.

  Meets Expectations: Competitive prices, the correct change, and a polite cashier.

  Fails Expectations: Excessively high prices, the wrong change, and a mean, obviously bored, or angry cashier.

- *Go to the restroom before the movie.*

  Exceeds Expectations: Spotlessly clean, roomy, well-lit, dry floors, well-stocked, nice decor.

  Meets Expectations: Clean, safe, and functional.

  Fails Expectations: Filthy, foul-smelling, broken toilets, missing hand towels, soap, or toilet paper, too crowded, too small.

- *Go into the theater and find a seat.*

  Exceeds Expectations: Spotless seating area; well-designed theater with no "bad" seats; enough light to find a good chair; pleasant background music or slides on the screen; roomy, comfortable chairs that recline slightly; drink and popcorn cup holders on each seat; a pleasant temperature—not too hot or too cold; no gum on the seat or sticky soda on the floor around you.

  Meets Expectations: Clean theater with good seats

nearly everywhere; safe, comfortable, and dark enough for you to enjoy the show when the lights go down.

Fails Expectations: Trash on the floor around you as you look for a seat, broken seats, missing armrests, sticky floors with gum everywhere, too hot or too cold, smells like cigarette smoke around you, a movie screen with a tear in it, loud music blaring from the speakers, gloomy lighting, burned-out exit door signs.

- *Sit and watch the movie.*

   Exceeds Expectations: A fabulous movie in a fabulous theater—great sound system, excellent film quality, no talkers or crying babies around you, and a memorable entertainment experience overall.

   Meets Expectations: A good movie in a good theater—good sound system and film quality, polite people nearby, and an enjoyable entertainment experience overall.

   Fails Expectations: A rotten movie in a rotten theater—shoddy sound and movie equipment; a terrible film print, out of focus or threaded in backward; talkers, smokers, and criers nearby; and an awful entertainment experience overall.

- *Leave the theater and go back to your car.*

   Exceeds Expectations: Friendly theater staffers who greet you as you leave, an easy trip through an uncrowded lobby, and a stroll through a clean, well-lit, and secure parking lot back to your car.

   Meets Expectations: No problems leaving the theater; a safe trip to your car.

   Fails Expectations: Rude theater staffers filing their nails, horsing around, or throwing food at each other as you leave; an uneasy trip as you're herded through a crowded lobby and out the door, only to find that your car is in a dark part of the parking lot, across the highway, or gone altogether.

When you look at these moments of truth individually and collectively from the customer's point of view, what connections can you make with your own experiences? In most instances, a trip to the movies usually meets our expectations. From time to time, something great will happen and these expectations will be exceeded; and rarely, we will experience a total service disaster. But by and large, we get our needs met satisfactorily.

When an organization exceeds our needs or expectations, we're pleased and often shocked. Since most of our service experiences tend to run at an acceptable level, it's a nice surprise when a company or an employee goes above and beyond the call of duty to make us feel special.

And when an organization fails to meet our needs or expectations, we're *displeased* and again, often shocked. Why? Because we've been conditioned over the years to expect good or at least acceptable service from the places we patronize. And it's an unpleasant surprise for us when a company or its employees goes out of the way to be rude, discourteous, or apathetic. Our mental customer report cards are sacred to most of us. We keep careful tabs on who treats us well and who does not. This reflects not only on our decisions about repeat business, but, equally importantly, on who we tell about that business and what positive or negative things we say.

Studies of customer satisfaction tell us that more people will discuss a *negative* service experience with their friends and colleagues than will talk about a *positive* one. Why is this the case? It's just human nature, I suppose. Further, since we're already accustomed to at least good service as a buying society, we usually only notice or complain if service is below our standards.

➤ *You mean to tell me that even if our company gives shining service to our customers, we might not get credit for it on the customer's report card?*

It's possible, but it's not something you should spend a lot of your time worrying about. To put it in biblical terms, excellent service begets happy customers who will give you high marks themselves, even if they don't rave about you to all of their friends. Some of them might—it's not unusual to hear people talk so much about a great service experience that you wonder if they're actually employees of that firm!

The point is that you can't always control what people say about your company. Positive feedback is always worth fighting for. The old Hollywood public relations adage, "It doesn't matter what they say about you as long as they spell your name right," does not apply to service businesses. Too much bad press can put you out of business.

Now that you've seen the cycle in operation, it's time to create separate Cycles of Service for your own organization.

CHARTING YOUR CYCLES OF SERVICE

➤ *Cycles? As in plural? There is more than one Cycle of Service going on in my company?*

Yes. There are literally hundreds or even thousands of these cycles taking place in your organization. The number largely depends upon what it is that you do or sell and how complex an operation it is to get your goods and services to the customer.

The Cycle of Service exercise is a good one to teach your frontline service providers, who may not have a concrete understanding of what their customers see and do when they come into contact with the organization.

Charting the various Cycles of Service is not a quick process. It involves several factors that are time-intensive and require you or your managers to get out and do some M.B.W.A., or Management By Walking Around. You've got to go out and look at your systems and processes with a careful eye for all the requisite details that go into each moment of truth.

Here are some suggestions that will help you identify the factors that go into each different Cycle of Service and help you create your own.

- *Start at the beginning, where the customer does.* Write down all of the important issues that strike you as you wear the customer's shoes for a day. Start with a rough draft of the Cycles of Service that interest you and make some notes about them. What are the first three things the customer has to do to come into contact with your organization? Drive to your building and walk in? Go to the counter and place an order? Meet a secretary at the front desk? Find a salesperson? Pick up the telephone and dial your number? Answer a mail-order ad?

   What is the customer's initial impression of your facility? If this is a phone transaction, what is his or her initial impression of your phone system? If it's a mail-order contact, what is the level of ease or difficulty it takes to contact you?

   Once inside or on-line with your firm, what are the individual steps the customer must take to buy your goods or services? What individual steps do your employees take to guide or hinder this process?

- *Get lots of help, advice, and feedback from your front-line service employees.* Be prepared to ask them questions and, more importantly, to write down their answers. You should be ready to take on the role of a "traveling suggestion box" as you roam the confines of your company with pen and notepad at the ready. As I have said, these folks are on the front line every day, working with an array of customers, meeting their needs, solving their problems, and, you hope, exceeding their expectations. They know what's what and can give you more information than anyone else about what goes on in your company and how it relates to the actions that result in service to the customer.

- *Create a Cycle of Service for each of the significant customer interactions you can identify.* Again, this is not something you can complete in an afternoon. Depending upon the size and type of your firm, you may have to draft a flock of helpers to give you the information, data, and organizing assistance you'll need.

Start with the simple circular design, create some "step" areas, and start filling in the blanks. Give yourself plenty of space, since you'll need to make additions, adjustments, and corrections as they come to mind. If you can get help from others around you, have them repeat the process with the cycles they have identified.

- *Update and adjust these cycles as conditions change.*

As with many parts of the quest for superior service to the customer, your identified cycles will be fairly dynamic operations. Things will change as the needs and expectations of the customers change. You need to stay on top of these cycles because they offer you the best look at your day-to-day customer encounters.

JUST WHO ARE THESE PEOPLE AGAIN?

Sometimes our search for the nature and operation of the many Cycles of Service in our organization can give us pause. The power of the cycles is not in clarifying what we already know, but in *revealing* what we did *not* know. Sometimes the creation of various Cycles of Service points to new questions about *who* our customers are and *why* they are.

These questions may pass through your mind as you work on the various cycles:

What are the factors that identify our customers?

Are they able to make a choice about dealing with our firm?

Can we make a choice about how and when we deal with them?

How has the definition of our customers changed in the last six months, one year, or five years?

What factors brought about these changes—positive or negative changes in our prices, product quality, or service quality; new products; market changes; global changes; economic, political, or local changes; additional value offered; new competitors who have come in; or old competitors who have left?

This leads to an even more perplexing issue, thanks to the ever-so-rapid changes in our technology. What you hailed as state of the art and leading edge just six months ago may look positively prehistoric today. And it's not just electronic technology that has changed, it's "service" technology as well. Some of us have become very skilled at serving our customers in new and shining ways.

▶ *How sophisticated are my customers about my products or services or even my industry or markets?*

As the personal computer revolution has proved, it may be necessary for you to educate both your new and existing customers before they can make buying decisions.

For all of the hype and fanfare surrounding the so-called information superhighway that is supposedly coming soon to a cable box or telephone line near you, a tremendous dollar investment will still have to be made by those companies that want access to the sanctity of your living room.

Since a good majority of us are not technocrats (as the running gag about the blinking "12:00, 12:00, 12:00" on the VCRs in this country suggests), someone is going to have to give us all an idiot lesson in how this technology will actually work and, more importantly, how it will make our lives richer than they are now.

Educating your customers before they buy is not uncommon. The insurance, investment, and financial planning community has been doing it—with varied success—for years. Perhaps the reason your customers are not buying from you is that they don't know *why* they need your products or, worse, that they don't know how to use them.

Maybe its time for a "chalk talk" of sorts. Part of any sales process, whether it's for a new chicken sandwich or a new bull-dozer, starts with explaining how to work (or eat) the darned thing in the first place.

THAT DIRTY WORD: COMPETITION

Paste the following axiom on any eye-level surface in your office or work area:

Whatever you're not willing to do to win and keep your customers, your competitors probably are.

While it may not be entirely grammatically correct, this phrase has what might be safely called a high "wince" factor, as in, every time you look at it and think about what you're not doing for your customers, you wince. Whether you actually shudder outwardly or not is up to you, but you can rest assured that your competitors are probably thinking about you as much as or more than you're think-ing about them. All of this leads to yet another important question.

➤ *How sophisticated are my competitors?*

In the grand scheme of customer care, satisfaction, and value, who wins the gold medal? In what areas do your competitors beat you? And in what areas do you excel over them?

Price? Location? Size, shape, or availability of your products? Warranties, guarantees, or price matching? More sale-priced items? Higher-quality products? 800-number telephone access? Service twenty-four hours a day? How are you different? How are you the same?

Don't take these answers for granted, assume you already know them by heart, or think your customers don't care. In the day-to-day operation of your organization, it's sometimes easy to forget the things your customers are thinking about you.

THE ADDED-VALUE SERVICE COMPANY

We've got low prices! We've got lower prices! We've got the lowest prices! The beat goes on, and the jingles all start to sound the same. But if you think the price issue is all your customers care about, you're wide of the truth.

Today, it's not just price that makes you competitive, it's service. There are other *value factors* that make the difference as well. And if your salespeople are constantly complaining to you that they can't sell your products or services because your prices are too high, it's time for a lesson in the other value factors for your goods or services. Remind them to sell using the following value elements that have nothing to do with price:

- Quality service to all customers
- Product quality
- Warranties or money-back guarantees
- Service or installation after the sale
- Industry leadership
- Reputation for quality from satisfied customers
- Reliability that extends through the company to the products and services
- Prices based on the total value of the product or service, not set arbitrarily or simply in line with the market
- The unique desire to do things right for the customer

Customer Value Criteria: What's Important to Them?

➤ *So if it's not just price, how do I determine these other things that are important to my customer? What questions should I ask?*

The easy answer is, "A lot of them." The hard answer is, "It depends upon your business." Certain things are more important to some customers than others, and some things should definitely be more important to you than others. For example, if you run a small supermarket, the freshness of your produce should be more than a bit more important than the color of your employees' work shirts.

The customer cares much more about quality food than about whether or not your people make a fashion statement. Having said all this, doesn't it sometimes still appear that business owners and managers spend their time focusing on issues that concern themselves rather than their customers?

This could be phrased another way: *company convenience over customer convenience.* As we have seen in our discussions of service systems (and the ones that will follow in Chapter 7), it's not *what's* important, but *who's* important. As the Cycle of Service has illustrated, it's not how you get things done that works for you, it's how you get things done that works for the customer.

CUSTOMER FEEDBACK: THE REST OF THE STORY

➤ *Okay, then* **when** *do I ask questions of my customers?*

When things are going well, when things are going poorly, and when things are just going. In short, yesterday, today, and tomorrow.

To quote an old marketing maxim, "The time to advertise harder is when business is bad, not just when business is good. In hard times, your customers need to know about your firm more than ever. Don't cut back, go forward."

It's the same in small-business life with your customers. The time to ask for feedback is when things are going badly, not just when things are going well. While you're busy trying to solve the trillions of problems that appear in lean times (as opposed to just the millions during the happy years), your customers may be trying to tell you what they really need. In effect, their feedback can literally save your business.

➤ *How about an example of this?*

Let's suppose you run a chain of plumbing supply warehouses.

You sell to the public, but the lifeblood of your business is the wholesale buyers: general contractors, plumbing subcontractors, and independent plumbers who buy large quantities of your materials for their use on construction jobs.

One of your best-selling items is plastic piping. You get this piping from one manufacturer and sell it in different sizes, diameters, and lengths. In fact, you sell so much of this material to these heavy-duty buyers that it accounts for nearly 45 percent of your total product sales.

Lately, however, your sales have started to drop off—dramatically, in fact. This troublesome sequence has started to cut into your profits, and you want to know why.

You start by picking up the phone and dialing up one of your largest customers. He tells you some surprising news: "Your plastic pipe is no good. We've used it on several jobs, and much of it has been defective. We just can't afford to make mistakes with our customers by using shoddy materials. Sorry, but we've been buying a different brand from your competitors."

Other calls to other customers reveal the same information. You've suddenly got a product quality problem on your hands. A check of your computers reveals another significant problem: high returns for—you guessed it—plastic piping.

When you talk to your employees, you hear the same things: "Yes, boss, we've been getting a lot of that pipe back, but we figured it was just a bad batch or that our customers were using it incorrectly. We heard the complaints, but we didn't want to bother you with them. We just made the refunds and sent the stuff back to the manufacturer. We didn't think it was that big of a deal."

Now you've got two problems, one that relates to product quality and one that relates to your firm's *systems* quality. Your customers are unhappy with one of your products, and your people don't recognize the consequences of their actions as they deal with your customers. They are either afraid, unwilling, or unsure of how to come to you with the elements of this growing crisis.

An important call to the manufacturer is in order. It's time to make the manufacturer aware of these problems, or change suppliers, to try and win back your customers. Once you've got new and better product on the way, you can change the way your employees respond to customer complaints and the way they keep you informed of potential problems with product and service quality.

This whole scenario begins and ends with feedback from the customer. The solution lies in how you gather that feedback, respond to it, and instruct your employees to do the same.

> *So how do I ask questions of my customers?*

Mingle with the customers

Working either as a recognizable employee of your company (in uniform, in a suit, etc.) or as a "hidden" shopper of sorts, walk and talk with the people who do business with you. Listen to what they are saying, and if you don't hear the answers to questions you have, ask them. You'd be amazed at how much a total stranger will tell you about your company if you just ask politely.

Work with your employees and observe first, how they get feedback from customers, and second, what that feedback means to them

Go ahead, get your hands dirty, so to speak. As you work with or watch your people handle the customers, see how they get feedback from customers about your products, services, and systems. Are they asking direct questions like, "Are you happy with our (product or service)? Is there anything else we can give you? Can we expect to see you again soon?"

This is obviously a short list, but if your employees are asking good feedback questions, they should at least be getting good feedback answers from many of the customers.

When time permits, ask your employees how they react to the customer feedback they hear. What does it mean to them personally? How does it affect—positively or negatively—the way they handle that customer or future customers? Do they have any suggestions to help improve the products, services, or systems?

Create good feedback systems and maintain them

A sheet of cobwebs covering the "Customer Suggestions" box can mean only two things, and both of them are bad: Customers don't know about the feedback system in your company and therefore can't use it when they have legitimate concerns, or customers know that their complaints and other feedback are going unaddressed, so they just stop saying anything. The trouble is, by that time you've probably already lost them.

If your written customer feedback materials need revision, fix them. If they're too small, too old, hard to read, or just not right, make them better, more accessible, and easier for the customer to complete and return. This last point gives many companies trouble. What's the use of having a well-designed customer feedback sheet if there is no means for collecting it? Asking the customer to leave it with someone at the front desk or to mail it in is not always practical or convenient for them. Create a designated customer response collection device and manage it from the start. These responses are (or should be) important to you. Don't let this collection process go unnoticed.

Monitor (or even listen in on) phone calls to your people from satisfied or unsatisfied customers. If you do follow-up phone calls to get feedback, listen as your employees interact with the customer. Make a few calls yourself and record the feedback you get.

Reward customers who fill out your feedback sheets, cards, or questionnaires.

Any legitimate customer who takes the time to fill out one of your comment cards deserves a reward. This could be anything from money-back coupons, free food or drinks, or a complimentary gift item. You can start by throwing away cards filled out by children, obvious psychotics, pranksters and practical jokers, or other people who don't deserve the opposable thumbs God gave us.

One of the reasons customer and employee suggestion boxes fail so miserably is because sometimes they're all sizzle and no steak. "We make suggestions or give our managers feedback all the time," says one frustrated hotel worker. "Nothing different ever happens. It's like they take the suggestions and complaints away and bury them in some hole outside."

At least once per month, you should compile all legitimate feedback you receive from customers or employees and report back to the people involved. If it's a customer problem and you promised to fix it, now is the time to recontact that customer and explain what you've done. If it's an employee or a systems problem, meet with the people it affects and discuss your changes, or better yet, ask for more feedback from them after you've implemented the new ways.

Whether it's good or bad, immediately follow-up on the data you receive.

One of the hardest skills to acquire in life is the ability to accept negative feedback. Even if the criticism is justified, it's still tough to have someone point out your failings. When you own or run a business, it's even tougher because you can feel as if you're being assaulted on all sides. Negative feedback can cloud your good judgment, i.e., "Because they don't like my company, it must mean that, by association, they also don't like *me*!"

You must steel yourself to be prepared for less-than-glowing reports about the way you and your service providers handle the needs of your customers.

Once you've accepted the possibility that negative feedback may appear from time to time, don't sit there stewing about it, make the changes. Go and see the employees who may have some complaints against them and discuss the complaints calmly and rationally. There are always two sides to any story, and, as we have learned, the customer is not always right.

For systems problems, don't leap to make arbitrary changes for the sake of doing something. Get some help from the people who actively use your service systems and then make a good decision quickly.

CUSTOMER-BASED PERCEPTIONS: IT'S NOT WHAT *YOU* THINK IS GOOD

Let's say you're staying in a hotel and you have an important business meeting the next morning. Filling out the card for your room service order, you check the box that says, "Deliver between 7:00 and 7:15 a.m." You then hang it on the doorknob as instructed and go to sleep.

The next morning at 6:45 a.m., as you're busy soaping in the shower, you hear a knock on the door. "Room service!" shouts the bellman with your tray in his hands. Climbing from the shower with shampoo still dripping from your head, you sign for your food and trudge back to the bathroom. "Sorry," he says. "Sometimes we get a little busy, so we make early deliveries to catch up."

The moral of this tale is simple: For your customers, sometimes early is just as bad as late. An early arrival means that you eat when you're not ready to, and a late arrival means that you wait to eat and thereby put the rest of your schedule in jeopardy.

Some small-business leaders make changes in their organization just for the sake of change. Others make changes based on what they *think* the customer wants or will buy rather than on what they *know* the customer wants or will buy. This is not to say that you need a crystal ball to make your business decisions and predictions, just that any important decision you make that affects the life of your company ought to come from research.

In other words, don't buy a big and expensive machine to make something the customer hasn't told you he or she really wants.

American car makers, who should know better, often fall into this trap. Instead of concentrating on developing a few strong products and competing with the Japanese on the basis of those, they throw a whole auto show at the customers every year and thereby confuse them.

The tossed-off line by the bellman in the room service story says it all: "It's not what's good for you, it's what's good for us." If that's the mindset in your organization, it's time for a big change in attitude.

Chapter 5

Building Your Strategy: A Formula for Service Delivery

"When patterns are broken, new worlds can emerge."
—Tuli Kupferberg

Since by definition a service strategy is "a distinctive formula for delivering service," this chapter emphasizes the need to define service value as something that is both important to the customer and deliverable by the organization. And sometimes you can have one without the other.

You've certainly seen this paradox yourself. Some companies think they know what's important to the customer, but are not able to deliver it, largely because of faulty systems, the wrong or untrained employees, or both.

Other companies may have good systems and good front-line service providers, but no idea of what the customer really wants, values, expects, or needs. This chapter explains how market research, focus group activities, and a thorough "scan" of the organization can help mold the service mission, vision, and values.

And as the fizzle factors have demonstrated, other firms may have middle management and employee support, but little or no support from top management. Consequently, any service program they try to initiate or any changes they try to make in the way the customer is served probably will fail.

And at the bottom of this pile is the company that has no clue as to what is truly important to the customer *and* shoddy systems *and* the wrong people on the service front line. These firms can't figure out which end is up. They fail on a number of counts, the most important of which is customer satisfaction—and therefore, customer retention—and in addition they suffer from the perils of bad management. They spend too much time racing around the grounds and seeking to blame the employees, the economy, or those "fickle" customers for their downturn in business success.

Many of these firms on the edge have failed to answer a single important question: *What business are we in?*

On its face, this sounds easy. For one thing, all of us are in the sales business. We sell things, either products or services, to people. But the deeper definition is often much harder to uncover. Besides knowing your business, the next most important question is: *What makes us tick?*

To discover this, you'll need to use what former President George Bush called "the vision thing." For our purposes, let's call it an organizational scan of the way your firm operates.

As pointed out in Chapter 3 concerning the elements of the Service Triangle™, the service strategy is based on three critical factors:

1. What's important to the customer (based on knowledge and feedback)
2. What the company is in business to do (the mission)
3. What's important to the company (the core values)

These days, what you *don't* know about what your customers want *can* hurt you. Successfully developing and adhering to your service strategy—involving these three critical success factors—will help you grow, survive, and thrive. Failing to identify and understand any of the three does your company, your employees, and your customers a disservice.

The Parable of the Fish

Here's a short object lesson to start things off, a service enigma, if you will:

The following interesting quote may or may not make sense, depending on how you look at it or whom you ask. It's bound to start your thought processes about whom you sell to, what you sell, and why.

This comes from the May 31, 1993, *Forbes* magazine. It seems that Mr. Charles T. Munger, vice chairman of Berkshire Hathaway, was musing over the misjudgments investors make.

He said, "This fishing tackle manufacturer I knew had all these flashy green and purple lures. I asked, 'Do fish take these?'

'Charlie,' the manufacturer said, 'I don't sell these lures to fish.'"[1]

As a small-businessperson with no desire to scare away or anger the paying customers, how do you take this quote?

This seemingly innocuous story has layers upon layers of service thought built around it and there is no right answer, but let's consider the different possible answers anyway:

- How would the professional fisherman, who earns his daily meat and spuds by catching fish in tournaments, take this quotation?

  "Does the damn thing catch fish? Yes or no? If it works, I'll use it. If not, I won't. I'll ask three of my colleagues if they use it. Or I'll buy one and test it. If it works, I'll take a gross of them. If not, it goes overboard."

- How would the serious, devout fisherman take this? This is the one who has the latest baits and tackle, gets up at the crack of dawn to go out on to the lake, and reads the solunar tables in the sports pages every morning to see when they're biting.

  "I think I might need one of those things. Does it come in

different colors, different sizes, or other shapes? Will it work on bass, trout, or bluegill? Are there any reviews in any of the magazines?"

- How would the weekend fisherman take it? This is the one who has a few pieces of gear and a small tackle box, and manages to get out onto the lake once per month?

  "How much does it cost? Is it on sale? Can I get a discount if I have a coupon? Will it fit in my tackle box?"

- How about the fishing gadgeteer and fishing hobbyist? He buys all the latest goodies, subscribes to all the fishing magazines, but rarely goes out to catch actual fish.

  He probably wouldn't care if it caught fish or not. "Hey! It's green and purple! This will look great in my tackle box! It's shiny and looks really great. Give me three!"

Would you buy a fishing lure from a manufacturer's rep who answered the question, "Do these catch fish?" with "I don't know. I'm not a fish." or "I don't sell lures to fish. I sell lures to fishermen. They can do what they want with them"?

Here's the moral to the parable of the fish: Is this an odd response to an honest question? Yes. Do we sometimes answer questions from our customers in a similar way because we fail to see things from their point of view? Yes again. As I discussed in the previous chapter, it's not what you want, it's what the customer wants. And in the tale of the fish, should it be what works on "hooking" the customer or what actually works on hooking the fish?

SELF-DISCOVERY: CRITICAL QUESTIONS, CRITICAL ANSWERS

To further help you create your own service strategy, you've got to figure out what business you're actually in. Take a moment and a pen and some paper to answer these questions for yourself. Your participation in this exercise should be a part of your ongoing organizational scan anyway.

1. What service or product do we sell?

2. Can I write my company's mission statement, core values, and beliefs on one page?

3. Can I tell people exactly what it is that we do in two sentences or less?

   (With respect to questions 2 and 3, brevity is the soul of wit, and it makes for easier explanations and service strategies too.)

4. Can I make an accurate guess about the service mission of my top three competitors?

5. How will I communicate our service strategy to my customers? To the leadership and management in the organization? To my employees?

6. If I were to look at this organization honestly, how would we rate today on the customer's report card?

7. If it exists at all and as we know it today, what is (are) our current:

   - purpose
   - size
   - mission
   - direction
   - vision
   - core values

The Last Five Questions for Your Organizational Scan

Who are we as an organization?

What are we as an organization?

Why do we exist as an organization?

Where we are headed as an organization?

How we are going to get there as an organization?

A Brief Customer Scan

There's obviously room for more discussion than this, but as they pertain to your service strategy, these questions should get purposeful answers:

> Who are our *core* customers?
>
> Who helps us keep the doors open every week?
>
> Do we have customers now that we never would have thought about six months ago?
>
> What about international customers?
>
> Who are they?
>
> How are their needs different from and similar to those of our U.S. customers?
>
> Where do we fit into the global economy even if we don't sell things overseas?
>
> Do we ask what our customers want, or do we guess?

A New Global Perspective for Your Strategizing

As you plan your service strategy definition statement, keep in mind that it should both serve your organization now and be able to serve it into the twenty-first century, which, at this writing, is only six short years away. The turn of our century, or the new millennium, once thought to be so far from view, is suddenly right around the corner.

This is not to say that your service strategy must be so carved granite that it's an immobile force for the next decade. As we saw in the early 1980s, exercises in long-range planning don't function too well at a time of rapid change. And for some small-businesspeople, it's hard for them to predict what will happen next month, let alone over the next five years.

While this shouldn't stop you from making thoughtful plans, it should help you put a limit on how much you can do in terms of guessing the future. Unless you have a fully functioning crystal ball, leave the predictions to the carnival fortune tellers.

For an exercise in future thought, think about what the year 2000 will mean to your business. How will things be different? How will things be the same? What changes in technology will make your job of serving the customer easier or harder? What will be the impact on your products or services, not just in the way you create them, but in the way your customers consume or use them?

Recall that most DOS operating systems for computers start or "boot up" their machines with the current date and time. So the date June 29, 1993 would appear as 06/29/93. Some software users, dealers, and manufacturers have asked, "If our systems are date-oriented in the twentieth century, what will happen when we have to enter the year 2000 as a last-two-digits number? The number 00 will screw up our accounting programs because it's not recognized as a valid date."

What was once taken for granted by the computer software customer is bound to become a new source of apprehension for the software folks who will have to fix this problem when it arises less than a decade from now.

There may be new machines, new electronic devices, and any number of new virtual reality gizmos that will improve the way we run our businesses and our lives. But even so, the key to the success or usefulness of many of these items will depend on whether they hinder or help you in meeting the needs of the customer.

As a number of 100-year-old or older U.S. companies can attest, brilliant technology and expensive electronics are not always necessary in order to stay in business. Today, Campbell's sells good soups, Nabisco makes good food, and Cracker Jacks makes good caramel corn snacks, just as they did 100 or more years ago.

Besides being industry leaders and pioneers, these firms and others like them have figured out what's important to the customer, what business they're in, and what makes the company go.

The unwritten motto of many long-time firms seems to be, "If something works, let's stick with it. Since we're in business for the long run, we'll find out what our customers want and need and expect and give it to them. At the same time, we'll orient our organization so that we have systems and employees built around these customer needs, not the other way around. We've been in business for 100 years or more *because* of our customers, not in spite of them."

LEARNING FROM THE BIG GUYS: SOME SUCCESS STORIES

➤ *I'm fairly sure I know what my customers want—low prices, good services, quality products, etc. Should I define it even more as I create my service strategy?*

While these things are all important—even critical—they are only part of the list. You've got to dig deeper and look at the intangibles too. Look at an example of the service strategy of Ben & Jerry's Ice Cream company. (If we're going to dissect an organization, we can at least pick one that's fun. Even Richard Simmons, Susan Powter, or Jenny Craig would get weak in the knees over a pint of B&J's best chocolate.)

On the surface, what is Ben & Jerry's service strategy? What is the company in business to do? The extremely short answer is three little words: Sell ice cream. But the bigger picture and its commitment to do this one thing points to other intangibles as well.

Let's look even harder, using the three service strategy criteria as a clue to more answers.

1. What's important to their customers?

We'll cut to the chase with this one. People like and eat Ben & Jerry's ice cream because it tastes good, but also because it is a *premium* ice cream product. This is not the plain-wrap, generic frozen goo you buy at the supermarket when you have to feed kids at a birthday party, this is a premium (read this as "expensive") ice cream.

Many people buy this brand because they like the unique flavors you just can't get with other ice creams, others because they like the catchy and punny product titles, and still others because they like the way Ben & Jerry's (as the label attests) supports Vermont dairy farmers and uses their milk products to manufacture their desserts.

But let's face it, Ben & Jerry's has positioned its products in what might be safely called the "yuppie" dessert-buying market. As with Haagen-Dazs, Frusen-Gladje, and the others of this ilk, some people will pay top dollar for an expensive ice cream in order to make a statement that says to all who will notice: "This is a pricy product. I can afford it. Therefore . . . (fill in whatever message about taste, sex appeal, power, or high finance you want)."

2. What is Ben & Jerry's in business to do (its mission)?

For one thing, sell gobs of ice cream, and for another, have fun doing it. While some companies still haven't figured out that it's possible to do both, the people at B&J's grasped this concept early and often.

Clearly, much of this is based upon the dynamics of Mr. Ben and Mr. Jerry as the founders of the company. As with most successful firms, their vision for the direction of the organization has infected the people who work there to the nth degree. The quality of worklife in the organization, as it's rated by the employees, is consistently high. The story about how the highest paid executives don't make more than seven times the salary of the lowest-paid employee has paid great morale dividends.

How about this as my own understanding of B&J's: "We sell high-quality premium ice cream to discriminating customers. It's made from all-natural ingredients and reflects our commitment to better taste, texture, and flavor and an overall 'fun' ice cream experience."

3. What's important to our company (our core values)?

See the first statement in point 2 again. While B&J's, like all good companies, wants to make money, its owners and employees want to enjoy themselves while this cash-acquisition process takes place. News articles, cheery pieces in the business magazines, and even TV segments all demonstrate one thing: "This place is a blast! We make ice cream for a living! And some of what we don't sell we get to eat!"

If I could hazard a guess about B&J's business values, it probably would cover the following factors:

- We want to sell lots of ice cream, but not at the expense of not having a good time while doing it.

- We want to provide the highest-quality products to our customers and still be able to make a profit while doing so.

- We are committed to the environment, especially in our local area.

- We are committed to small businesses, especially in our local area.

Put those things together with the mission and you have a good working definition of a powerful service strategy. While it's not necessary for you to copy another company's strategy to the letter, you can learn what the good firms feel is important and see if those same issues apply to you.

Definitions of Spirit Mixed with a Strategy

Herb Kelleher, CEO of Southwest Airlines, is widely known as an innovator and as an aggressive marketer of his planes and his people. What started as his young upstart Texas airline is now nearly twenty-five years old. His spirit is seen is his message. It's infectious, and his employees (and many of his long-time passengers) practically worship him for it. He has a no-nonsense Texas style of communicating what is important to him and his airliner:

We started back in 1971 with three planes serving three Texas cities. In the short-haul markets most people will drive those distances instead of fly. A lot of people figured us for road kill all the time. But today we've got 144 planes in 34 cities. We like mavericks—people who have a sense of humor. We've always done it differently. You know, we don't assign seats. Used to be we only had about four people on the whole plane, so the idea of assigned seats just made people laugh. Now the reason is you can turn the airplanes quicker at the gate. And if you can turn an airplane quicker, you can have it fly more routes each day. That generates more revenue, so you can fly more routes.[2]

Look how much information Kelleher reveals in this short paragraph that actually serves to highlight his airline's service strategy.

He tells when his firm began, how small it was, how he recognized a niche among a specific group of customers, how he had to face the slings and arrows from skeptics who thought he would fail, his steady plan for growth, the people he likes to employ to fulfill his service strategy, and the reason behind some of his customer-friendly systems.

That's a whopping chunk of lore about a highly successful firm that started small and grew steadily, all the while following a service strategy that says, "We won't try to compete head-on with American Airlines or United. We will offer a carefully identified group of passengers our low fares, convenient departures, and friendly staffers to help them achieve their travel objectives."

Mail meter king Pitney Bowes also has this same public sense of how to describe its service strategy to its customers. It has taken the time to quantify what it feels are its customers' most important concerns and questions. By referring to what it will do to make things right, it adds an extra element, a personal touch, to its strategy that confirms the message: "We care about our relationship with you. If you have problems with our equipment, we will act on them, and fast."

A follow-up letter sent to customers after they've received a new postage meter tells the customer, "We will work with you and for you, now and later, to make sure you are more than just satisfied. We want to exceed your expectations because we recognize the important parts of the day-to-day relationship between our customers and our machines":

Pitney Bowes Mailing is committed to providing our customers with the finest products backed by the highest quality service and care.

Our five-year guarantee means that if you are not satisfied with the performance of any of our products, we will replace it at our expense. If we provide a replacement product and it does not fully perform according to specifications, we will promptly give you a full refund. You will have no concerns after you acquire this product.

You can always count on timely customer care to make sure that the product has been delivered and installed on time.

We will answer your telephone calls and written communications promptly, fully, and courteously. Your billing statements will be easily understood and accurate.

Our Customer Satisfaction Guarantee means that your problems are our problems and will be resolved promptly. In short, it means no excuses from Pitney Bowes.[3]

Is this not the most complete, soup-to-nuts service strategy statement in creation? This outstanding missive allays fears, answers questions, covers concerns, adds value, and tells the customer, "Go ahead, use our products with complete confidence in them and us. We will not let you down."

It's Time for Your Service Strategy: A Template for Success

Think of your own service strategy as your operating plan for how you deliver service to your customers. Here's an example:

Let's say you operate a chain of Japanese fast-food outlets, like the "rice, chicken, and sauce in a bowl" establishments you see in many shopping malls around the nation. Here's one way to describe your service strategy in the form of a mission statement:

Our customer and market research tells us that people like convenient and well-known Japanese dishes. We cater to busy lunchtime customers like businesspeople, students, parents with children, and workers, shoppers, and tourists on the go. Our locations are near busy shopping areas, large office complexes, or well-traveled freeway exits. We offer value-priced, high-quality, good-tasting Japanese "takeout" food to our customers using a convenient walk-up order window. We use innovative and environmentally safe packaging to keep the customers' to-go orders hot and fresh until they arrive back at their destination. Our spotlessly clean indoor dining area allows our customers to eat in comfort. Our prices are fair and competitive, and our menu items are carefully reviewed each month, based on suggestions from our customers and our employees. We will guarantee to replace any food item that is not properly prepared free of charge or refund the customer's money. We are a service-driven firm, and we pride ourselves on our ability to meet our customers' needs and exceed their expectations each time they visit us.

What do we know, in terms of its service strategy, about this fast-food chain?

- Its decisions about food, price, location, clientele, etc., are based upon *research*, not accident, happenstance, or blind luck. It has used hard data to make hard decisions. In one form or another, it has asked important questions of its future and current customers.

- Its statement tells its employees what the company is in business to do. It mentions price, quality, taste, and adaptation to the food needs of the customers as keys to the company's success.

- The statement declares that the company is devoted to the management and delivery of high-quality service to its customers.

In less than one page, this fast-food outlet has summed up its entire service strategy and then some. In clear, concise, and unambiguous language, it has said what it takes some companies thirty pages to say.

Worse, it says what some companies *never* say to the supposed leaders at the senior executive level, the senior and middle management staff, or the front-line service providers, or, more importantly, to the customers.

Do you think that any new employee, regardless of his or her status in the organization, age, or work experience, could read this and *not* understand this restaurant's core message?

For the sake of our workforce and the future of our "on-growing" service economy, let's hope not. But we can safely assume that even a new front-line employee with no job experience could read these words and figure out what is important to this company. Good service strategies shouldn't require a postgraduate degree to read or even write.

And once this message is in place, whether it's in the new employees' handbook, in the policies and procedures manual, reprinted in the company newsletter, or posted on the walls of the kitchen or corporate offices, it serves as a learning tool and a constant reminder: "This is our service strategy. This is why we are in business. This is what we hold near and dear to our collective hearts."

You should be able to look at the service strategies of our friends at Ben & Jerry's, Southwest Airlines, Pitney Bowes, and our imaginary Japanese takeout restaurant and instantly recognize some parallels with your firm, even if you don't make ice cream, plane tickets, postage meters, or fast food. The elements of *your* message are built into these examples. Take what you can to make one for your own organization.

FINDING YOUR NICHE AND STAYING THERE

➤ *Okay, I understand the reasoning behind a well-defined service strategy, but what do I do with it once I've created it?*

Service strategy clarity starts at the top and flows through the organization. What you do from your "executive," "management," or "business owner" desk affects what goes on at the front line.

The message you send—the strategy your people understand—goes a long way toward helping everyone understand what your business is really all about. And the first step in this creation process starts with discovering what's important to the customers—not just what they will pay for, but what they *want* for their money.

The December 6, 1993 issue of *Forbes* magazine featured an article about McDonald's and how the folks under the golden arches were highly disturbed because their fast-food restaurants were not filled at the dinner hour. One Mickey D's executive went on to bemoan that the company was losing ground to the pizza delivery chains, and that although McPizza had not tested too well, it was still under consideration. The piece also discussed a McDonald's TV ad campaign that used the theme "Pick up dinner here on your way home from work and you can spend more quality time with your kids."

Still, even with the glitzy ads and the wide expanse of food choices on the menu boards, Ray Kroc's legacy still loses out as a serious dinner choice.

A letter to the *Forbes* editors in the January 3, 1994, issue put a firm finger on the pulse of the problem. Reader Ern Kovacs of Naperville, Illinois said,

> McDonald's will learn sooner or later that it can't be everything to all people. One of the strengths that built its success was a simple menu served fresh, hot, and fast. Today it is difficult to find an ordinary cheeseburger on the menu. The elegant simplicity of the original concept developed by Ray Kroc has given way to a virtual army of bureaucrats and regulations. While continued growth in untapped foreign markets will mask [McDonald's] ailment for a time, some major adjustments in its strategy is needed to sustain its leadership in the domestic market.[4]

A similar theme was addressed in a June 1993 article in *The New Yorker* magazine, discussing how New York Times newspaper publisher Arthur Sulzburger Jr. put the concept of strategy bluntly to his management team. In describing a three-day gathering designed to discuss issues, create new opportunities, and fix existing problems, he said:

> The purpose [of our meeting] was to test our assumptions as to what we really were, what we really stand for. If you go into any process of re-creating an organization, you better damn well have agreement as to what can and can't change. What is it that we hold sacred?[5]

Your organization's service strategy should tell you, your employees (at all levels, but especially the front-line service providers), and your customers what you hold sacred.

Notes

1. "Other Comments," *Forbes*, May 31, 1993, 22.
2. Copyright 1993, American Express Corporation.
3. Copyright January 28, 1994, Pitney Bowes Corporation.
4. "Readers Say," *Forbes*, January 3, 1994, 12.
5. "What Young Arthur Wants," *The New Yorker*, June 28, 1993, 61.

Chapter 6

Instilling Spirit: Employee Service Empowerment

"People need responsibility. They resist assuming it, but they cannot get along without it."

—JOHN STEINBECK

Like a house built on a weak foundation, even the best service company will tumble if the support people don't hold up their end. Employees have to be told what is expected of them and then given enough leeway to make decisions that can help both the customer and the organization. This also can be expressed by the phrase "Become your customers' agent," which means "Do what you have to do to help your customers get what they need, solve their problems, and 'wow' them from time to time."

When you teach people how and why service is the one intangible item that keeps the paying customers coming back for more, they will respond with renewed efforts. This is especially true the sooner they realize that the performance and health of the company is tied to satisfied, returning customers.

This is not a hard lesson for some employees to learn; others never learn it, no matter what you say or do. It's like that old joke about thirteen-year-old paper deliverers being the backbone of any successful daily newspaper. When the Circulation Department head says, "If that kid doesn't hit your porch with our paper every morning, we're in trouble!" he or she is not too far off the mark.

The business owners or executives can't be everywhere and can't do everything, including serve every customer that comes through the door. You must be able to rely on your front-line people and their managers and supervisors to get the job done.

And the nearer to the top you are, the farther away you are from the customer. If you're a business owner or operator and your firm is past the infancy stage of its development, you probably don't have much of a direct-contact "hands-on" connection with the customer any more. Unless the customer is an old and true friend or a long-time, loyal client, you may not even see him or her any more unless you're called in to mediate a problem.

In the early start-up phases of any organization, the leaders thrive on this sense of closeness to the customer. But success and expansion can move you out of this realm and into the ethereal heights of management, leadership, and decision making.

And as we will see in Chapter 8 on spreading the message throughout the organization and asking your people to carry the torch, the farther you get from the customer, the more it requires you to have the strategy, systems, and service people already in place to continue what you and the other business leaders have started.

But just because it's true that as the firm grows and adds the mandatory layers of management, departments, and work units it needs to function efficiently, it's still hard for many start-up or early-stage veterans to give up the ship and move on to other duties. While it sometimes may feel as if the inmates are running the asylum, this is a natural part of the small-business evolutionary process.

In his "At Work" column in the San Diego *Union-Tribune*, business reporter Michael Kinsman, speaking of the growing move toward more employee empowerment, said it best:

> To many executives, this is a discomforting topic. It means a surrender of power and an acknowledgment that the people who make the widgets, sweep the floors, and run the daily computer reports are as essential to the success of the company as those with offices in the executive suite.[1]

Commenting on this, Mr. Owen Gaffney, who spent thirty years as an executive with the Polaroid Corporation, said,

> Many, if not most people who hold positions of authority or power will relinquish or share that power only with pain, anxiety, and fear. But sharing that authority is a prerequisite to having employees step up their commitment to the company.[2]

In other words, if you're not willing to let the horse have its head once in a while, be prepared for a bumpy pony ride. Empowering your front-line, supervisory, and middle management people should not be the same as giving the keys to your vintage Corvette to your newly licensed sixteen-year-old. Service empowerment for your employees is not an all-or-nothing proposition. You don't say, "There you go. Take care of all the customers and their needs. If you want anything, ask someone else because I'll be in my office."

Just as the founders of any small business took a hands-on approach to every segment of the business, they must now take the same hands-on approach to enabling, training, and guiding the people around them. A customer-powered business centered around the service quality imperative does not run on autopilot.

THE GOLDEN RULE OF SERVICE EMPLOYEE TREATMENT

What does it mean if you're a "tough" boss, a "tough" manager, or a "tough" supervisor? It probably means that you're no fun to work with or for. Some company leaders and managers have failed to learn the lesson that you get more work out of people if you reward them when they do well. You just can't motivate front-line service employees in the Clyde Beatty circus lion-taming fashion—that is, with a whip and a chair. Nowhere is this more apparent than in service industries that have a built-in high turnover rate of front-line people anyway. It's no personnel mystery that the employees who work for retail stores, for fast-food outlets and mid-range restaurants, in banks, and in semi-skilled manufacturing jobs tend to move about at will. The long-time worker is more rare (and more of a luxury) in these industries than in others.

If your firm falls into the high-turnover category for whatever reason, it makes no sense to try to frighten the troops with threats of termination—there are three other companies across the street that will hire them.

This leads us straight to the *Golden Rule of Service Employee Treatment*, which says, "Do unto your service employees as you want them to do unto your customers." If the adage about reaping what you sow has any truth to it, you've already seen this rule in action on both ends of the scale. Treat your employees like adult workers with real feelings, wants, needs, and concerns, and they will model a more positive outlook and attitude with their customers. Give them a sense that they have a say in what goes on and that their opinions about the operations and procedures are important and they will work hard for you.

Treat them like spoiled children who are always one step away from being punished for indiscretions, fail to consider their feelings in your decisions about what they do and how they do it, and they also will model a certain attitude with your customers. Make arbitrary, reckless, or ignorant decisions about their work, don't bother to give them any feeling that what they say or do matters, think that empowerment is a category reserved for the top brass, and they will help you run the company into the ground.

If you recall the classic 1984 comedy *Ghostbusters*, Bill Murray finishes berating Annie Potts, his secretary, just seconds before she answers a phone call from a bona fide customer. Her piercingly shrill yell, "Whaddya want?" into the receiver tells us how she feels about her particular service job as well as her boss.

➤ *How about difficult employees? How do we treat them?*

The same way as you treat your easy employees: with respect. Clearly, however, you'll need to invest more time in guiding or training your difficult employees to be more team- and customer-oriented. This can be time-consuming and tough, but with extra patience you can turn an average employee into a great one. Just don't expect anybody to respond if you treat him or her like dirt, like a commodity to be managed, or like an easily replaceable machine part.

This is not to say that you have to love everyone who works with or for you. You just have to be willing to treat them well. And you have to be able to tolerate the different ways people do their jobs and have supreme patience with and understanding of every employee who demands it. And this is also not to say that you have to organize your company as if it were a Club Med. There is a wide gap between managing a sweatshop in which employees are docked for every slip-up and running a pay-for-play outlet where employees waste your time and dollars on two-hour lunches and long telephone chats with their friends.

You can run a tight ship with a no-nonsense attitude about laziness, or any other of the seven deadly sins, and still be respected for your ethics, fairness, and managerial humanity. You should start with solid employee systems in place—that is, a policies and procedures manual that is fair, balanced, well-written, and not thicker than the New York City phone book. You or your personnel and HRD people should communicate to any new or current employee what it means to work for your organization.

In today's civil suit-happy society, there is a real need to take new service employees if not by the hand, then step by step through your service-quality program and say, "This is what we do to serve the customer. This is the part you will be expected to play. This is your role and job duties. Here is how you handle unique problems the customer may bring to you. This is how you communicate your needs to the managers and supervisors near you."

There is a huge difference in the way front-line service employees do their day-to-day work, treat their customers, and even have the desire to go the extra mile for them or you if they feel appreciated, heard, and given the chance to ask questions, make suggestions, or change systems for the better without the fear of reprisal.

To a considerable extent, whether your people help or hinder the customers starts with how they feel about your organization. A high quality of work life and a sense of ownership in the organization can change hesitant employees into champion service providers. It never hurts to remind yourself of the Golden Rule of Service Employee Treatment, especially on those bad days when it seems like everything your employees touch breaks, leaves, or turns to stone.

➤ *What are some good rules of thumb in terms of better employee treatment?*

It's often the small things that make a difference. You wouldn't want to be berated for your mistakes in front of your colleagues, so why do some supervisors make a big production out of on-the-spot discipline sessions that make everyone feel embarrassed, angry, or contemptuous? And while the proper place for counseling, constructive criticism, or discipline is behind closed doors, what's wrong with some hearty praise in front of everyone now and then? Nothing can brighten an employee's day like a verbal pat on the back for a job well done in front of his or her peers.

How you treat your employees is a reflection of your company. And the employee treatment loop comes full circle to the customer. It doesn't take your customers too long to understand the culture of your organization. If the employees feel respected and empowered, the customer will hear about it through their actions, words, and deeds. And if the converse is true, the customer will know that too.

HOW AND WHY TO HIRE GOOD SERVICE PROVIDERS

As odd or even inhumane as this may sound, one of the few benefits of all the "downsizing" that has been taking place in many service industries is that there are a lot of great people out there now who need work. Since ours is a service economy, there are always going to be companies looking to fill service jobs, and at present they have more applicants than they need.

This plethora of talent gives you a number of choices as you look to fill key positions in your small business. And one thing that small-business personnel types may fail to keep in mind is that since these companies are not IBM-sized, they just can't hire the wrong employee at the start. Perhaps it helps to think of your small business as more like a family. You have to work together, you may have to eat together, and you have to spend a significant portion of your waking hours in the same building, in the same office, or in the same room. Therefore, you had better get along with one another and each of them had better be able to do the work he or she was hired to do.

Frankly, service positions are unique in many respects as jobs because of the burnout factor. It's just plain tough to handle customers for eight or ten hours a day. Different jobs—especially in retail industries—certainly illustrate this fact. It takes more than a little emotional maturity for the service employee to cope with the stress, deadlines, and myriad of customer-related issues that face him or her each working day. This is the primary reason why you need to hire the best service people you can afford: The job can be demanding, and you must have people who can meet the challenges.

This means that your company has to interview thoroughly, look at past work experience, and judge the person on the basis of several important factors:

- Does this person have the training, experience, qualifications, and background that will make him or her right for a service position?

  A careful and thorough interview and hiring process will help you answer this question. These days, even if you're hiring someone for the most junior, lowest-skilled, or lowest-paying position in your firm, you have to ask just as many questions and do just as many background checks as you would if you were hiring someone for a management position. Taking shortcuts just to fill service jobs is a mistake that could have painful consequences for you, your other employees, and your customers.

- Does he or she have the right service skills and mental and physical stamina needed to handle our customers each day in a pleasant, efficient, creative, and even thoughtful manner?

Ask anyone who works in a store, hospital, restaurant, or telephone-order center if he or she is mentally and physically tired at the end of a working day. The best employees are the ones who are just as sharp and just as committed at the end of the day as they were at the beginning.

- Has he or she demonstrated the ability—either through past work or life experience or during the interview process—to think creatively, problem-solve on the customer's behalf, and deal with difficult episodes or customers?

  Any interview with a new service employee should include some scenarios that ask the person to think a bit outside the usual boundaries to solve a problem or add value for a customer when a situation arises. While you want your people to follow rules of behavior and action, it's okay to give them the confidence they need to help the customer in ways that aren't always written in the employee manual.

- Does this person have the winning service attitude that is critical to winning the moments of truth on the customers' report cards?

  This last element strikes me as the one that can tip the scales in an applicant's favor. I'd bet that an employee with real enthusiasm and an attitude that says, "I can do it, no matter what it takes," but with less job experience will work much harder than someone who has lots of service experience, but no fire in his or her eyes and no determination to become the customer's need filler and problem solver.

HOW AND WHY TO FIRE TERRIBLE SERVICE PROVIDERS

Notice the operant word here is not *bad*, but *terrible*. There's quite a difference between the service employee who's having a bad week and the one who is just not right for the job. Terrible front-line service people do more than just give bad service to their customers; they also poison the people and the relationships around them. Besides harming your customer relationships, these rotten eggs can alienate their coworkers, irritate their supervisors and managers by their inability to change their behaviors or improve their attitudes, or just treat the customer in a way that is inconsistent with the high standards of the organization.

And this poison effect can seep into vendor relationships, into internal customer interactions, and even into your best workers' personal lives. Nobody likes to work around a grouch, and if your coworker is truly toxic, his or her bad attitude can spoil your day, make it no fun to come to work, and in effect, rub off on the customers you serve.

➤ *So what's the answer? Just fire the bad ones and be done with it?*

Not necessarily. In the worst cases, with front-line service employees whom you or your managers feel are completely unsalvageable, you probably have no choice but to let them go. But in other cases, it may not always be necessary to give up hope. Why not move them to another place in the company?

The conversation could go like this: "You know, Dave, we've been getting a lot of customer complaints about your work. Some of your coworkers have told us your attitude is bad, and it seems like you don't enjoy your work with customers. We'd like to give you another opportunity. Is there any other place in this company where you would feel more productive?"

And perhaps, if the employee does not want to be fired and can make a real commitment to the organization, he might say, "Yes. I'm glad you asked me this. I don't feel comfortable dealing with customers and their problems every day. I'd really like to work in the X Department. Could I transfer to there?"

If this happens, you've saved an employee from termination, replaced him with someone who is more suited for the job, and saved your customer relationships at the same time. Sometimes by giving a difficult employee a sense of empowerment that says, "I can control more of my destiny here," you can save a career that was originally headed for the scrap pile.

> *What if that doesn't work?*

Sometimes a bad fit is just a bad fit, and a job change, several discipline sessions, or lots of conversation about attitude adjustments or work performance will not fix the problems. It's time to terminate someone who refuses to be a team service player. In a small business, you just don't have the luxury of keeping a bad employee. However, large firms can substitute people who can fill in until a new employee is hired; if you have a small workforce, you probably don't have that option, so your people will have to work extra hard to take up the slack left by a termination.

People should be terminated for two reasons: There is not enough work for them to do, or they are unable to follow attendance policies, work conduct rules, or work performance rules. While they or you probably can't control the first situation, the responsibility for the second rests squarely on the shoulders of the employee.

Attendance policies should be a clear part of your policies and procedures manual. Work conduct rules are also an important part of the manual, since they describe what can and can't be done on the job, e.g., no smoking in the dynamite storage room, no soda pop cans near the computer keyboards, etc. And work performance rules, which may be different for each job, should spell out what is acceptable and unacceptable behavior as well as how, when, and why work should be completed.

You should feel more comfortable about your discipline and termination policies if they follow these three criteria. However, if we realize that the world can be divided into three groups in terms of compliance, "yes," "no," and "maybe," people, sometimes you just have no choice about letting someone go.

- *Yes people.* They work hard, offer feedback when asked, make good suggestions, take feedback and criticism positively, and get along well with the customers and their co-workers. They follow the attendance, work conduct, and work performance rules within your guidelines.

- *No people.* They fall into the opposite categories from the yes folks, and if they can't or won't change, get rid of them. You shouldn't have to beg your employees to be good to the customers. After you've trained them and told them what you expect in terms of their service job performance, the responsibility for working hard for the customer falls squarely on them. No terrible habits, awful attitudes, caterwauling, rationalizing, or whining should be permitted.

- *Maybe people.* They are on the borderline, so you'll need to give them more of a reason to become yes people. It takes something other than just a paycheck or great company benefits to motivate them to work hard for you and the customer. What is it? Maybe a different job in a new area? Maybe more or less responsibility? Maybe they need a partner to team up with so that each works twice as hard as before? Maybe they need more help, training, hands-on supervision, or positive feedback from you? Maybe they just need to vent? If they're still good workers, maybe they need to be moved to internal customer service positions. Whatever it is that they want or need, it's part of your job to find it out. If you want to make the effort to help them become yes people, give it a try.

No "Emotional Alimony" Allowed

It's common for some CEOs and other executives to keep long-time employees on full pay even though they now fail to pull their own weight. This is especially true in small-business operations, where the long-time employee is also a "charter" member of the organization.

This person may have been in the trenches with the rest of the starters in the early days. It's common for him or her to feel entitled to certain treatment that other people with less time on the books do not receive. In the worst case, this can lead to a number of quandaries, including a sense that the long-time employee is just coasting along, taking advantage of you or your policies, failing to complete assignments that others must do, or wasting your time and money on efforts that do not help the organization.

In a lot of these cases, a showdown is inevitable. As with any other employee, you have to start with informal counseling, move to more formal discipline procedures, and then consider termination as your only alternative should the change you request not happen. If you can honestly say, "Although this person has a long history with this firm, he or she has continually failed to do what we have asked," then you really have no choice but to let the person go. Keeping deadwood—no matter how long it has been there—is unfair to the rest of your more hard-working staffers.

HOW AND WHY TO CREATE A SERVICE SWAT TEAM

While the title may be a bit misleading (there's no need for guns), the principle is the same. Why not create a small cadre of front-line service people who can function as a roving information and feedback-gathering group? The idea is twofold: Give your front-line people more of a sense of empowerment by putting them in motion around the organization, and, equally as important, let them gather the valuable information you need to make planning choices, decisions, strategy adjustments, system changes, and even employee modifications.

Take some of your best employees, even if it's just two of them, and give them the responsibility to go out at intervals and collect information about your systems and your employees. Let them ask questions of their coworkers or even people with whom they do not work, every few weeks, once per month, or every quarter.

You'd be amazed at how much information several committed employees, armed with pens, pads, and a penchant for good questions, can gather for you. This information comes right from the front line and can really help you and the rest of top management make adjustments in the way all of you treat your customers.

If you have enough personnel, you may also want to consider making your "Service SWAT Team" available to your customers as well. As an example, Haworth, an office furniture company, has what it calls its Customer Satisfaction Team, who are trained to answer customer questions at any time before, during, or after the sales process.

> ➤ *What should the team members ask their coworkers?*

Depending on the products or services you offer, the questions will differ, but here's a sample of a few things that you will want to know more about:

> How's it going with our new or current systems or methods?
>
> Do our procedures help you work well with the customer?
>
> Are you running into any snags that need fixing?
>
> Are there any recurring problems that we should know about?
>
> What kind of new systems can we create to make your job easier?
>
> What help do you need in terms of materials, equipment, or machinery to make your job easier?
>
> Do you or your work group need more help, additional training, or extra, specific help from management?
>
> What kinds of customer feedback do you hear?
>
> What kinds of problems do customers tell you about?
>
> Give us some examples of shining moments with customers or of your coworkers who have handled their customers well.

Do you have any stories about customer interactions that would help the other people in this company?

What works well in this company?

What does not work well and should be changed?

What kinds of additional training do you think would help you or the people around you?

How about your internal customer relationships?

Do you have any systems problems—on either side—with the people who help you serve the customer?

Is there anyone who works behind the scenes for you and the customer who does an exceptional job?

Who are your service stars?

What do they do (not just their job duties) that make them service stars?

Who are the leaders in your unit, team, department, or group?

Are they visible or hidden?

How should we reward the people who do a great job serving our customers?

And the need for this roving response team is not just limited to the front-line service people. As I'll discuss in Chapter 8, a *management* team can be just as valuable. Your managers and supervisors can gather different kinds of information, which can come from their unique perspective. Getting feedback and information from both levels of the organization can go a long way toward helping you decide your next direction.

The Difference Between Service Management and Fad Management

Part of the point of service employee empowerment is that it can change the way employees perceive the overall management commitment to any service quality program. In other words, they will not buy into anything if they don't see the leaders of the organization doing the same. As our previous look at fizzle factors illustrated, a lot of noise and excitement in the beginning is great, as long as it's followed by equal helpings of real work and movement.

Service management is certainly a powerful concept, but *focused* service management is what really breeds success in your firm. And focused management, which takes a single, driving concept and uses it as a road map for the organization, is vastly different from what is fondly called "churn" management. In this regard, churn management changes things for the sake of changing them, thereby helping to rattle people into thinking that their jobs or their duties are not safe from excessive executive tinkering.

Just as you shouldn't buy into every management fad that comes down the pike without doing the prerequisite research that must accompany any significant change, your employees expect you to do the same with new service quality programs. New does not always mean better. Further, this continuing "fad road to failure" serves to dishearten the employees who must suffer the course of each roller-coaster ride management has mapped out.

An article in the *Wall Street Journal* discusses how this problem has taken root in a number of large and small companies. They bounce from program to program, either changing when things start to turn bad or not letting the employees get comfortable with new roles, new duties, and new approaches to the way they work.

> Companies that promise employee participation and control but then do not change the locus of power are vulnerable to worker disenchantment," says Laurie Bassi, an economics professor from Georgetown University. While she believes such changes are needed at many corporations, she admits, "If they are just words, people who have put their hearts and souls into believing get jaded; it makes it harder to introduce the next thing.[3]

For a small business, it's too expensive and time-consuming to try one quick fix after another. It damages top management's credibility and sends the wrong message to your employees, who are looking for both guidance and the ability to work in a self-directed manner. It pains them to hear: "This is the one big program that will turn this company around," and then, "No, wait! *This* one is really the program that will make a difference," or "Okay, those others weren't really that significant. *This* new one is the real deal!"

People don't like to work for companies that play musical chairs with service programs. You know the drill: The music stops and everybody scrambles to find a seat aboard the new program. Too many moving parts or too many demands make people uncomfortable. They want to know where they fit, what is expected of them, what they can do to improve their job, and what they can do to improve the customer's experience, which ultimately makes their job better anyway.

➤ *Keeping all these fads in mind, what's the best way to initiate a new service quality program?*

Before you start with the nuts-and-bolts issues—strategic planning and thinking, systems changes, and new roles for service employees—you have to ground your employees with what your organization really stands for. This is why the first and last service message you teach and preach should sound the same:

> Here's what we're all about as a company. Here's what we sell, offer, and provide for our customers. Here's what we do as service providers to meet our customers' needs and exceed their expectations.

The benefit from any top-notch service quality program—one that focuses on a solid service strategy, customer-friendly systems, and highly empowered service employees—is that it is far easier to teach and preach company wide than any of the new fads coming out of the bookstore shelves, business school diploma factories, or magazine pages.

IF YOU WANT EMPLOYEE EMPOWERMENT, REWRITE THE RULE BOOK

As our politicians like to remind us, "Your government works for you." Some of our more forward-thinking elected leaders have even started using the word *customers* instead of just calling us *taxpayers*. But one of the reasons many employees who work for the government don't feel like they're in the service business is because the rule books are so thick. "How can we serve the people who call us or come through the doors when there are so many do's and don'ts associated with our jobs?"

If you've ever worked at any level of the government or served in the armed forces, you know that bureaucracies feed on paper. And whether it's the government or a service firm, too much paper and too many rules can turn good people into drones, not creative, responsive workers. The phrase "I can't do that for you because it's against the rules" should be stricken from the lips of your service providers, their supervisors, and your policies and procedures manual. It's not what the customers want to hear, and, believe it or not, it's not what your employees want to say to them. They want to help their customers, and too many pages in the rule book can stop them in their tracks.

As you look at your company's P&P manual, do you get the initial sense that it's customer-friendly for your employees? They're *your* customers; they belong to you just as the outside customers being to them. And since your job is to serve them so that they can serve your customers, a careful review and edit of the P&P book is a good way to fine-tune a continuing employee empowerment process.

As you review the pages, ask yourself, "Does our P&P book create policies that hinder our employees' abilities to serve the customer or not?" If it's three inches thick, unreadable, or too restrictive, you may be stifling the creativity of your people.

➤ *Do I want "creative" employees? Wont they get into all kinds of mischief if they're given too much leeway?*

There's always a balance to everything. Empowerment is all about giving your service people opportunities and procedures they can use to shine and the ability to balance what they *can* do with what they *need* to do.

What you may discover is that by giving your people the responsibility of becoming the customer's agent, they can often come up with creative ways to serve the customer. And this creativity doesn't have to break any laws, rules, or organizational policies in the process.

"Breaking the rules" to help the customer is not as dangerous as it sounds. Where is it written that your service people must deliver things on their off-hours? What about the salesperson at your furniture store who says to the customer, "You live right near me. Since your car is already full of the lamps and coffee table you just bought, why don't I drop off these couch pillows you ordered on my way home?" Where is this documented in your P&P manual? It's probably not there, and frankly, your customers don't care if it's written anywhere, as long as they get their needs met.

Should the waitress at your steakhouse tell her customers to try the new dessert shop next door because they have great pastries and coffee? Is she driving down your dessert business or adding value to the experience of eating at your restaurant? Again, this is not written anywhere, it's merely something extra that helpful service people want to do for their customers. Just because it's not written in the rule book doesn't mean that it doesn't exist or that your sharper employees aren't thinking about it.

Find some room on your mental bulletin board for the following "rule-buster."

We don't use four-letter words around our customers—like "We can't do that," "That isn't our policy," and "We don't make the rules here, we just follow them."

These are things your customers don't want to hear and your service employees don't want to say to them. Problem solving, not buck passing, should be the order of the day.

Big Brother or Better Employees?

With the year 1984 now a decade in the past, George Orwell's vision looks fairly remote. But the concepts he created in that work—most notably "Big Brother Is Watching You"—have carried over into many of our present-day discussions of control, supervision, and, in some cases, surveillance.

The use of the "electronic boss" to keep tabs on service employees is a hot topic in many newspapers and business publications. Employee labor unions have their opinions, management has its own, and the employees who are subject to scrutiny—via computer, from managers who listen in and monitor their customer calls, or from even video cameras that count the number of times they go to the bathroom or the coffee pot—have many strong things to say about the need for "corporate eavesdropping" on the job.

This brings up several pro-or-con questions: Do these monitoring techniques help or hinder the way the front-line employee serves his or her customers? Does the information gathered from listening to employee-customer phone conversations serve as a useful feedback tool or as a way to "ding" problem workers? And does this watchdog process make the front-line employee feel comfortable or apprehensive?

According to the National Association of Working Women's group "9 to 5," up to 26 million members of our workforce are watched by cameras, computers, or supervisors as they perform a wide range of service activities for and with customers.

In an article discussing the issue, both sides of the process were debated:

Some, such as union leaders and advocacy groups, have publicly decried such workplaces, calling them "electronic sweatshops," places where constant monitoring from often remote sites supplants good management, invades a worker's right to privacy, and triggers stress-related health problems. Says Louis Gerber, a union representative for the Communications Workers of America, "Too many employers practice the credo 'In God We Trust; on employees and customers we spy." Others, including many in corporate America, consider electronic monitoring . . . a valuable tool for assessing, improving, and rewarding on-the-job performance and assuring [service] quality.[4]

It's easy to see the points made by both sides, but as with many service-system improvement methods, the real test starts with the employee and ends with the customer. If you use sophisticated employee monitoring at your company, does it make for better frontline service people? Do your employees find it threatening to the point of physical discomfort, or is it just not that big an issue? Are you taking heat from your employee groups, labor relations gadflies, or the American Civil Liberties Union, or is it just another part of the work at your firm?

And equally as important as the mental health and well-being of your service employees, have these methods improved your customer relationships? Has your data pointed to any success stories or reasons to commend good systems and good people? Has it shown you things that need immediate fixes or long-term changes? In essence, has the data collected by monitoring processes helped you and your employees serve the customer in a way that makes them necessary?

Many managers and even some employees feel that the whole issue has been blown out of context and is really no cause for alarm on either side.

"I like it," says a customer service telephone operator at a large HMO in Philadelphia, "It keeps the reps on their toes, [and it tells us] to say the right thing and speak to the customer the right way."[5]

Federal Express has been using various telephone monitoring systems for over ten years now. The package shipping giant uses "side-by-side" monitoring, where a supervisor sits next to a customer service rep, and electronic monitoring, where a supervisor can listen to calls from another site. The company insists that the information also serves in a bit of a carrot-and-stick capacity, helping managers know who should get merit raises and promotions. Says Paul Anderson, the managing director of customer service for Fed Ex Chicago, "We try to catch the employees doing something *right*."[6]

If this issue touches your small business, weigh the results in term of its effects on your employees and your customers. If it only helps one and not the other, what good is it?

AN EMPLOYEE EMPOWERMENT MISSION STATEMENT

Some companies just talk about employee empowerment, and others really do something to demonstrate it. This mission statement for the Embassy Suites hotel chain makes broad mention of the employee as the agent for the guest's pleasant stay:

> Whether you are joining us for business or pleasure, we want your stay to be a memorable experience. We take great pride in our facilities, our attentive and friendly service, and the spirit fostered in our team mission statement: We will set the standard for superior guest service by empowering our team members to ensure guest satisfaction. Our guest will experience a clean, comfortable and secure environment, while receiving an exceptional value. We will maintain an uncompromised position of integrity in community, corporate, and employee affairs. All of this we guarantee.[7]

In this example, the customers know what to expect, and the employees know what is expected of them. The statement highlights the concepts of teamwork, service employee empowerment, and just doing what it takes to make things right for the customer.

THE TRAINING CONNECTION: GOT NO TIME FOR THE LITTLE RED SCHOOLHOUSE ANYMORE

If the people in your organization don't have the proper or necessary training, job experience, or life experience to become highly service-oriented, give it to them.

If you're in charge, give your training department an immediate mandate to give you an operational service training plan. It doesn't have to be wall-to-wall from the start, but it had better have provisions for training everyone at the different levels of your organization.

And make sure the material matches the audience. It's perfectly acceptable and even advisable to have your executives, managers, and supervisors all go through the same front-line-level training as your day-to-day service providers. It's important for them to see how the front-line people serve the customers, and it's equally critical for the front-line employees to *see* top management spending time in the same classrooms as they do.

But it doesn't work in reverse. Depending on your industry or employees, the front-line people may not have the education, background, maturity, sophistication, or even the desire to sit through management-based training.

As companies such as Home Depot, Wal-Mart, Dunkin' Donuts, McDonalds, and Burger King have discovered, it's good for the "suits" to get out of the office once in a while. And if, as a part of their training experience, you can get them to roll up their sleeves and get into the classroom or, more importantly, out on the sales floor and face-to-face with the customer, so much the better.

Just keep in mind who your target audiences are and match the level of sophistication of the training to them.

If you're in a training position or if this is one of your work functions, be ready with a schedule of programs to give to your senior executives. Also be ready to go to bat for these programs if you feel strongly about them. One of the more maddening procedures that seems to emanate from the Training Department is what is often called the curriculum-based needs assessment approach. Here, the training manager simply writes up a list of class titles, each with a very short description of the class content, and ships it memo-style around the organization.

If lots of people respond to the memo, the training manager will schedule the training classes. If not, it becomes, "Oh, well, I guess nobody's interested."

This procedure of running it up the flagpole to see who salutes is wrong on several levels: It wastes time; it distracts from the training function; and it puts the responsibility for training back onto the shoulders of the employee or the managers rather than on the training manager, who should be in the best position to evaluate the courses and pick the ones right for the employees, not the other way around.

Your options for any service quality training program can start small and grow as the program itself matures. These include the following:

- *Face-to-face training at the worksite.* This is done by the managers and supervisors on an individual employee basis. It can follow a well-designed training plan that emphasizes three or four key points, ideas, or new policies the managers want their people to understand and use.

- *Role-play training.* This works well in a classroom setting, with some employees playing the part of the customer and others playing their own role of service provider. Sometimes seeing how the other side thinks, feels, and responds can help everyone determine what the customers' needs are all about.

- *Small-group training while on the job.* This can come from the manager or the supervisory level and can consist of a fairly quick review of existing policies, new ideas, and new systems to make their work easier.

- *Classroom seminars lasting from one-half hour to one week.* Whether these are facilitated by in-house trainers, outside training consultants, senior managers, or senior employees who can serve as trainers for their work groups, the seminar experience should not be taken lightly. It offers a powerful way to teach a lot of information over a relatively short period of time, in a controlled environment.

- *Manager-guided training classes.* These can consist of classes led by senior managers for specific managers of work teams, departments, divisions, or units. Like the seminar format, this training process can cover lots of material in a short time. And by using a manager as the instructor, you can improve the continuity between the material and the employees who participate in the training.

- *Supervisor-guided classes.* Like the above, these can consist of classes led by senior supervisors for specific supervisors of work teams, departments, divisions, or units. Some front-line employees feel more comfortable being taught and trained by their direct line boss rather than by a company manager.

- *Ranking front-line employee-guided classes.* If you have some gifted senior front-line employees, you may be able to draft them into service as trainers for their work groups. Some people feel more comfortable learning from their coworkers. Depending on the material to be covered and the audience, this can pay good dividends, especially in terms of employee empowerment.

- *Outside training consultants.* The benefit of using outside professional trainers is that they can often take a "helicopter" view that allows them to see issues and problems in your organization that may not be so apparent to you. Further, many of these people offer state-of-the-art training in service quality in a packaged program that you could not feasibly develop on your own.

    On the other hand, you need to establish a relationship with a trainer who will work with you prior to any training to understand fully the needs of your company. A trainer who tries to "parachute" in a few days beforehand with a one-size-fits-all seminar is usually a waste of your money and your employees' time. A good service training program should offer you many specific benefits that you can put to use immediately.

EVEN IF YOU'RE NOT THE OWNER, IT'S STILL WHAT YOU DO FOR YOURSELF THAT COUNTS

Writing in the June 1993 issue of *Playboy* magazine, columnist Asa Baber makes some rather pointed references about how to survive and prosper as an *employee* in the service revolution. His words make good sense for any employee (including you, if you don't own the small business where you work) who wants to convert himself or herself from just another employee to someone that the company needs, almost to the point of not being able to do without you. Baber says:

1. *Knowledge is king. You are what you know, so read and learn.*

   Think of the service economy as a knowledge economy. Most employers don't give a damn if you're male or female. What the business world wants is educated, knowledgeable, rational, effective people. People who fit more than one limited job description. People with multifaceted skills who can be moved from place to place within an organization. Smart, shrewd people.

2. *Economic sophistication will not get you fired, and it might get you promoted.*

   Let's face it: There's no room for amateurs in any profession. Capitalism has won the day, and we are all . . . tightly connected across international boundaries. So learn the rules of the game. Do you know how [economic change] affects your job and your market and your bosses and your wallet?

3. *Learn more than one trade.*

   Make a list of your job skills and start expanding it. How much training have you pursued in other areas, how many courses and seminars have you attended recently, and how many professional contacts have you cultivated?[8]

Given our fluctuating economy and amusement-park-ride job market, this is no time for any employee to feel too complacent. According to data collected by the American Management Association, in companies with 100 or fewer employees, 69 percent of positions cut in 1993 were held by salaried professionals.[9]

The "downsizing" numbers break down as follows:

- Middle managers: 33 percent
- Hourly employees: 31 percent
- Professional and technical managers: 23 percent
- Executive-level managers: 13 percent

Asa Baber's advice should be heeded by employees in any service-driven organization who want to get ahead and better themselves, not just the managers and executives.

Notes

1. Michael Kinsman, "It's the *How* of Employee Ownership That's Key," San Diego *Union-Tribune*, Oct. 1, 1993, p. C-1.

2. Ibid.

3. Fred R. Bleakley, "Many Companies Try Management Fads, Only to See Them Flop," *Wall Street Journal*, July 6, 1993, p. 1.

4. Lini S. Kadaba, Knight-Ridder News Service, "Orwell's 1984 Vision Comes True a Decade Later," San Diego *Union-Tribune*, Oct., 12, 1993, p. E-3.

5. Ibid.

6. Ibid.

7. Copyright 1994, Embassy Suites Hotels.

8. Asa Baber, "This Ain't No Party," *Playboy*, June 1993, 40.

9. "Up Front—Small Isn't Always Beautiful," *Business Week*, April 4, 1994, 8.

Chapter 7

The Added Value of Customer-Friendly Systems: Empowering the Service Organization

"The man who removes a mountain begins by
carrying away small stones."

—CHINESE PROVERB

Bad systems can kill even the most enthusiastic employees. They
also can drive away your customers in droves. If your organization
has too many "no" barriers in the way, your people can quickly
lose faith in what might otherwise be a good service program. It's
also more than a little hard to serve customers when there are so
many brick walls along the way.

This chapter will help you take a long, hard look at your organization to see which operational policies do more service harm than
good. Highly motivated employees surrounded by helpful systems
can make for a winning combination that benefits the customer, the
people, and the organization. Of course, the converse is also true.

The best working definition for service systems is "the way we
deliver service to our customers." This broad pass takes into account all the little and big things you do to help your customers get
the products and service they want, with a minimum of fuss, er-

rors, wasted time, and raised blood pressure. The operations—physical, procedural, technical, and even mental—help your front-line people provide for the customer.

Ordering a pizza over the telephone and having the delivery driver bring it to your house in under an hour is a perfect example of service systems at work. There are systems set up at the order desk, at the pizza maker's table, and with the delivery driver and his or her pizza-mobile. Plenty of behind-the-scenes effort goes into getting you the correct pepperoni-and-mushroom pie in a reasonably short period of time.

As the customer, your only real concern is if these systems *fail* to deliver your dinner. As the business owner, operator, or manager of the pizza restaurant, your real concern should be the strategy, the systems, and the people who get the pizza out the door and to the customer while it's still hot, fresh, and subject to a repeat sale the next day, week, or month later.

As the Cycle of Service examples in Chapter 4 pointed out, it takes a lot of little things done right along the way to give customers what they want.

And just as you took a hard look at the moments of truth in your organization's various Cycles of Service, it's time to take an even harder look at the *way* those moments of truth are created through service systems.

Your Systems Don't Have the Luxury of a Bad Day

If you'll recall from our definition, *moment of truths* involve pleasant interactions, in which the customer sees something positive about your organization, or unpleasant ones, where the customer comes away with a negative impression of some or all parts of your operation.

Obviously, positive, successful moments of truth are far more desirable than negative, unsuccessful ones, but the bad ones can do more harm than you may realize. It's no longer possible to chalk it up to experience and say, "Well, we just had a bad week. We'll win that customer back next time."

With the number of competitors at its highest level, prices at their lowest, and margins at their tightest, you just don't have the luxury of a bad day anymore. You've probably guessed by now that the phrase "Customers can be fickle" is closer to the truth now than it ever was in the past. You have less room for error now because, with so many choices and so many other companies competing for their attention, customers are just as happy to give someone else a try, especially if you have "wronged" them with some obvious service gaffe.

Worse yet, surveys and studies of customer responses, attitudes, and feedback tell us another terrifying but understandable fact: More people will talk about bad service experiences (in effect, failed moments of truth) than will talk about good ones (successful and probably unnoticed or taken-for-granted moments of truth). Word of mouth can be one of your best allies or one of your worst enemies.

➤ *You mean that if people have an especially unpleasant service experience, they will tell more people than if they have a good one? That doesn't make sense.*

On its face, you're correct. But think about your own life. If a friend or colleague tells you he wants to eat at a certain restaurant and you know that the food is good and the service is acceptable, you'll probably give it a passing thumbs-up. But if you've eaten there in the past and were given inedible food and lousy service from a plate-swinging cretin or cretinette, you're bound to give the place a hearty tongue-lashing. The rule of thumb when evaluating a service business seems to be: Good service gets a brief mention or no comment and bad service gets a lengthy tirade describing the litany of service crimes committed against you.

It's a sad but true facet of human nature, and you'll just have to get used to it. More importantly, you'll have to adjust to it and turn bad service episodes into good ones.

So, since your employees are human (unless you singlehandledly own and operate a robot factory), you're going to have bad days where everything goes wrong for the customer. You're also going to have days where no matter what you and your employees do for or say to certain customers, it's still going to *look* like everything is and was your fault. But remember, the customer is *not* always right. He or she may just want you to meet some needs. And those needs may be visible or invisible. It's up to you and your front-line service providers to bring them to light.

> ➤ *This sounds a bit bleak. You're saying that if my customer's "report card" indicates that we've blown a number of critical moments of truth, he or she will go elsewhere. What can I do to prevent this?*

There's no need to abandon hope all ye who enter here. Before we look at your systems and how to fine tune them, let's discuss a service idea that is so basic as to be ignored by some organizations. It offers you the best, fastest, and most practical way to correct glaring service system errors, failed moments of truth, and other signs of customer distress.

SERVICE RECOVERY: THE GREAT ERASER IN THE SKY

There is a way to fix even the most severe service foul-up and still keep even the most unreasonable customer relatively happy. It's a concept known as *service recovery* and it can really create a noticeable difference between you and your competitors.

To put it simply, service recovery is exactly what it sounds like—recovering a failed service moment of truth with the use of two simple words: "I'm sorry."

Nothing irritates a customer more than to be treated to poor service, for whatever reason, and then not to hear those fateful words from any service employee in the vicinity. Service recovery is really that basic: You or your people should apologize when the situations warrants it. It's amazing how far the phrases, "I'm sorry we made a mistake," "We apologize for any inconvenience we've caused you," or the best answer, "I'm sorry this happened. What can *I* do to correct the problem?" will go.

The moments following a service screw-up of any magnitude are critical to the customers. What you do right then *for* them means a lot *to* them. Your fervent actions to correct their problems play a large part in their decision to return and do business with you again. Now is not the time for rationalizations ("We couldn't help it"), excuses ("It was somebody else's fault"), or apathy ("Sorry, that's not my problem, my department, or my mistake").

Your customers want and need you to help both of you to recover skillfully and gracefully. When you do this well, you win friends, and when you don't do it well or don't do it at all, you make enemies. An example of what *not* to do in terms of service recovery—that is, absolutely nothing—will help tell the tale:

A Service Recovery Horror Story: The Hotel from Hell

As a business traveler, I have the opportunity (or curse) of spending many nights a year away from home and hearth. My enthusiasm for these trips largely depends upon the duration of the trip, the number of time zones I must cross, and the relative comfort of the hotel I've chosen. If you've traveled on business or pleasure, you probably have your own favorite cities, hotel chains, and types of rooms. But after several years of trips that start with planes and taxis, and suitcases (and the weary traveler) thrown face down onto a hotel bed, and end with suitcases, cabs, and sprints down the jetway, the act of travel gets old.

And unless you're staying at a true five-star establishment, one business-oriented hotel starts to look like the last one. For the most part, they all are reasonably priced, offer the same comfortable accommodations, and have a few amenities sprinkled in to help you remember them. And unless something disastrous happens, your memory banks probably don't recall anything significant. However, there are exceptions to every rule, and here's a story about one of them.

Last year, I planned a four-day stay at a Los Angeles hotel that is part of a well-known nationwide hotel chain. I had been to this same hotel many times before for business and vacation trips. I was even on a nodding basis with some of the staff. On this trip, I checked in Tuesday afternoon, lugged my belongings to the top floor—ten floors above the firmament—and began work on a project that would keep me in Los Angeles until Friday.

Imagine my discomfort when, at 3:30 a.m. Wednesday morning, the fire alarm went off for the entire hotel. As I staggered into my bathrobe and headed for the door to begin the long walk down ten flights of stairs to the street, a metallic male voice came over the intercom in my room and said, "We are experiencing some difficulties with the fire alarm system. This may or may not be a false alarm. We will notify you as soon as we know."

This news was followed by silence—save for the ringing of the fire bells—for the next thirty minutes. During this time, I packed my most valuable belongings, got dressed, and sat on the bed waiting for word.

After it had been confirmed that there was no smoke, no fire, and no need to continue ringing the alarm, our little fire drill officially ended. This was followed by the polite announcement, "We have determined that there is no fire emergency in the building."

As I reversed my packing, dressing, and pacing and climbed back into bed, I clearly remember saying aloud, "Why didn't he say, 'We're sorry for the inconvenience' or 'Please accept our apologies for this interruption and try to get a good night's sleep'?"

Rising early but not brightly the next morning, I continued to wonder why no one from the hotel desk staff had bothered to apologize for their intrusion. I understand that on occasion, fire alarms do go off in hotels, and most of the time they're not valid. But where were those two words—"We're sorry"—that would have sent us all back to sleep with more pleasant dreams?

On Thursday morning, the fire alarm waited until nearly 5:00 a.m. before again ringing throughout the building. Again with the dressing, again with the packing, again with the cautious peeks through the door as I looked for smoke, flames, or men wearing rubber boots, metal hats, and asbestos coats with their names stenciled on the back.

And again with the same metallic speech—sans apology—over the intercom. Having giving me the luxury of an additional extra hour and a half of sleep, I suppose they felt that an apology for this second night's inconvenience just wasn't necessary.

As I crawled out of the shower a mere hour later, I thought, "This couldn't have happened *two* nights in a row, could it?"

But wait, it gets better. (Not three nights! "How could this have happened?" you ask yourself and me.) On Friday morning, the hotel people decided to readjust my rapid-eye movement sleeping patterns by scheduling the next false fire alarm for 2:00 a.m. This time, I didn't pack, pace, or dress. I lay in my bed and said, "In about one minute, a man's voice is going to come over the intercom located strategically over my bed and tell me they're experiencing yet another false alarm." And so he did, and so it goes. As I packed to leave a mere six hours later, I decided to mention this unwanted floor show to the day manager.

Standing at the front desk with my suitcases, I quietly explained that while I could forgive one night, three nights of ongoing fire drills was ridiculous. To my dismay, my comments were met with a shrug of the shoulders and Speech 47, which starts with, "Well, these things happen" and finishes with "It's really not our fault."

In my haste to escape this House of Lost Fire Drills, I made an error I can only attribute to sleep-deprived bleariness. When I arrived home from Los Angeles and unpacked my luggage, I realized that I had left some of my clothes in the dresser in my hotel room. Since only a few hours had gone by, I called the front desk and explained my mistake to the same day manager. He promised to send a maid to gather my shirts, swim trunks, and socks, and have them sent by UPS back to me.

Now remember, this was the fire drill hotel. After one week, I called back. Where was my stuff? Oh, we'll find it and send it right down to you. Two weeks later, I made yet another call to the hotel. Any sign of my clothes? Oh, yes, sir, we're having them packed up and shipped to you.

To make a short story long, two months later, I received a large box from the hotel at my home. With relief and no small amount of exasperation, I opened the box to find—oh joy!—clothes. However, these clothes were not mine. The hotel must have rummaged through the lost and found bin and sent me everything they had. There were men's clothes, women's clothes, and children's clothes, none of which had ever belonged to me.

I repacked the box, shipped it back up north, and gave up hope. I also changed hotels, forever.

GIANT STEPS: A PLAN FOR YOUR SERVICE RECOVERY SYSTEM

The hotel story illustrates what I call the Popeye Principle, which occurs when the customer finally says, either silently or aloud, "That's all I can stands 'cuz I can't stands no more."

Here, he or she has reached his or her limit of human tolerance. And while this threshold varies from the extremely impatient to the supremely patient customer, it's still your job or your front-line employees' job to intervene when necessary to correct service problems with a healthy dose of on-site recovery. This does *not* mean that you or your employees must subject the customer to smile-training patter or foot-shuffling servitude. You can always be professional as you deliver an apology if one is called for.

➤ *It seems like there are so many ways things can go wrong. How I can I possibly "recover" from all of them?*

Remember that the concept of service recovery is such a simple, basic one that we often take it for granted in the hubbub that comes with trying to solve customer problems.

Add this one to your bulletin board of must-have service program quotations:

- *Problem with your product?*

  Use a service recovery plan to fix or replace it and tell the customer what you will do to make it right. You or your people should be able to use the good systems at hand to give the customer a replacement product with a minimum of hassle.

- *Problem with one of your service systems?*

  These are the many procedures that help to guide your customers, your employees, and your organization through the course of doing business together. Initiate a service recovery plan to adjust or do away with that system in order to solve the customer's problem. Make sure you tell him or her what you will do, what your front-line people will do, and what your organization will do to make it right.

- *Problem with one or more of your front-line employees?*

  This could be anything from a good worker who is just having a rotten day to a rotten worker who is doing business as usual with your customers. If you have an employee problem that directly affects the moments of truth with your customers, be prepared to intervene or have a manager or supervisor intervene on behalf of those customers. Again, tell the customer what you plan to do to make things right.

➤ *The common thread here seems to be that service recovery is really about telling the customer what actions you'll take on his or her behalf. Correct?*

While the phrase "We're sorry this happened" is a large part of the service recovery process, it will appear to the customer to be only so much eyewash if changes are not imminent. As we have seen with service programs in general, movement not backed by real change is mostly worthless. With any service recovery opportunity, the customer wants and *expects* you to do something now or in the near future to make things right. Merely apologizing and moving on to someone else won't do it—at least if you expect the customer ever to do business with you again.

You probably can confirm this last statement from your own experience. Every company and its people make mistakes; customers understand that. How those mistakes are rectified is what matters to the customer.

If one of your waiters spills soup on a nearby diner's suit, service recovery says that you apologize for the unfortunate accident, clean him up as well as club soda and a light dose of elbow grease will allow, and make an immediate offer to pay his food bill and his dry cleaning costs.

If a customer comes into your auto parts store with a broken or defective air filter, the right thing to do is replace it on the spot and, if time and the situation permit, help him or her to install it while the car sits in your store parking lot. Now is not the time to ask the customer to fill out a claim form to be sent to your Dallas, Texas, warehouse, along with the bad part and a copy of his or her driver's license attached.

People can be vastly patient, but if you continue to set things up to make it easier on you than on them, they're bound to protest. If they don't say, "Why do I have to go through this? It's not my fault all of this happened in the first place" to you or your employees, they'll say it more noticeably with their obvious absence at your company from that moment on.

SERVICE RECOVERY MEANS NEVER HAVING TO SAY "DO IT OUR WAY"

The old saw that says, "We're bigger, so we're better" doesn't always apply with service quality, and the concept of service recovery (or the lack of it) demonstrates this from time to time. Good companies, regardless of their size, history, products, or people, make good on their promise to be the customer's advocate or agent for change. By taking ownership of the customer's problems, when and if they arise, they do two things: They give the customer some sense that an actual living, breathing, and thinking human being has taken physical custody of his or her problem, and they protect the customer from some of the nightmarish service systems that plague some companies.

The only thing worse than a service problem that is not solved with a service recovery action is one in which your customers must perform their *own* service recovery steps to solve *your* problem. In effect, bad systems make for bad recovery opportunities. This happens whenever you ask or force your customers to jump through your systems hoops to get what they want. It's not fair, and it's not right.

To bring an example into play, it's necessary to name names. In the multilevel marketing industry, few companies can rival the success story that is Amway. This billion-dollar Ada, Michigan, company runs rings around its direct-marketing counterparts in terms of size, history of reliance and stability, product diversity, product quality, and even cost of goods. Amway's established and growing network of stars has attracted many converts across the country. In Japan, Amway is almost a national religion. Since most Japanese find it difficult to say no, be rude to salespeople, or turn down a request for their business, the direct marketing approach has had legendary success there.

But as we have demonstrated in places, might does not always make right. Large companies can fall into a bureaucratic rat's nest that smaller companies can avoid through careful planning.

Let's look at a story involving the return of an Amway product. It seems that a new Amway salesperson sold an expensive leather briefcase to one of her early customers. The customer had picked the briefcase out of Amway's expansive products catalog—a tome that rivals the old Sears catalog for its heft and vast number of different categories. The order went in, and the briefcase arrived by mail soon after.

At first, the customer was very pleased with the briefcase—until the bottom split and the handle started to come off. Since the product had failed within only a few months of work, it was still under warranty. The Amway rep asked her "upline" leader—the man who started her in his chain of Amway salespeople—for a refund/return form. He said that he didn't have any of the necessary forms and that she should just call the Amway toll-free number and they would send her a batch of them.

To her surprise, the Amway telephone operator said, "We'd be glad to send you a pack of damaged product return forms. Should we put this on your credit card?"

"Credit card?" she asked, confused by the request. "I just want some copies of the form I need to return a defective briefcase. You mean to tell me I have to *pay* for a piece of paper that will allow me to replace one of my customers' broken products?"

"Oh, yes," came the reply from deep in the heart of Michigan. "We do not provide product return forms free of charge. You'll have to buy a set of them."

This is lunacy! Amway asks its own customers to pay for the privilege of returning a defective product! This is a systems problem staring it in the face. I'm fully aware of how the multilevel industry operates. And I'll even agree that in certain industries like this one, there is no such thing as a free lunch. But who ever heard of making the customer pay for something that should make his or her service experience better? With this pay-for-paper system in place, Amway is actually punishing the very people it should be supporting.

The lesson to this story lies in its impact on you and your organization. Look around at the systems that affect both your customers and your front-line people. How often do you put either of them into this kind of nonsensical position?

It's time for another set of mental bulletin board messages:

---

1. Don't make your customers follow your service recovery rules.

They won't understand why or how they need to do this, they won't like it, and they probably won't do it more than once. If certain approaches or systems are not working well or are failing to meet the needs of customers, when called upon, don't be afraid to throw out the old rule book and create new methods for solving problems and meeting needs. Recovery is about making wrong things right, not about continuing to perpetuate the same errors or mistakes.

---

2. Make it easy for customers to participate in the process of fixing any problems, correcting any errors—no matter who caused them—and come back to your organization with the idea that even if things go wrong, it will be easier than they expect to make things right.

Just the fact that you and your customers are in a service recovery mode in the first place can be a stressful experience for both of you. When things go wrong—whether we are customers or service providers—we tend to slip out of our comfort zones. Now is not the time to force the customer to march in a zigzag line from A to Z when he or she is already disappointed or disturbed about some aspect of the business relationship with you in the first place.

---

3. Don't make your front-line service people struggle through customer- and employee-unfriendly systems that make it hard or impossible for them to solve their customers' problems, or become their agents for change.

Just as it's tough on the customer to fill out innumerable claim forms to return a broken toaster at your appliance store, it can be just as taxing for your employees to make them waste their time and effort on outdated, ill-thought-out, or just plain dumb systems for product returns.

It's not just getting one customer a new toaster that's important, it's the repetition of this same systems process that your employees must travel through with the customers that came before and the ones that come after.

As with many service ideas, the best solutions and systems suggestions can come from the people who are on the front-line with the customer every day. Don't hesitate to ask for feedback from your employees on all of your customer-based systems. They want things to go smoothly with the customer just as much as, if not more than, you.

> *What can I do to make sure our systems are customer-friendly and employee-friendly? Is it even possible, given the number and scope of the service systems that we already have in place?*

Recall from our discussion of external and internal customers that the people behind the scenes who may not see the customer face to face still have two duties: to get their own work done, and to assist the front-line people as they deal with the customers. Your inside systems should be just as user-friendly for these internal customers as your outside systems are for your external customers. It should be possible and even desirable to make changes, corrections, or additions to each without causing too much uproar with either side.

For this to happen with any degree of certainty or success, you need to get back into the customer's moccasins again. No matter what product or service your firm sells, delivers, or provides, you've got to be able to say, "We've experienced what the customer sees when he or she comes into contact with us, and we've witnessed certain things. Looking at everything we do, these service systems work well for our customers and these don't. Let's improve upon the good ones and replace the bad ones."

Here's a message from one of the small business brethren, Mr. Tom Severance, director of the Entrepreneur Center and chairman of the business department at MiraCosta Community College, a two-year school in Oceanside, California. In terms of your service systems, he says:

> Small businesses need to change their mental approach. Look at [your company] from customers' eyes and [ask yourself], "What would make them want to buy our products or services?" Most small business people don't look at it that way. They may manage their product or service well, but they fall short in marketing it to the customer. Small business owners need to think of "market orientation" instead of product orientation. The goal is to acquire and maintain customers.[1]

And this sense of walking a mile in your customers' shoes as you experience what they do in terms of your service systems can be taken quite literally. Many large and small firms make frequent use of "mystery shoppers" concept. For all of its critics (mostly insecure employees who feel that they are being spied upon), this "customer for a day" approach to testing service systems is an excellent way to gather data, to see what works right and what fails, and to see how your employees use the systems they have in front of them to serve customers, correct problems, and encourage or discourage the notion that your organization is a customer-powered business.

Whether you use a mystery shopper service, as many retail establishments do, or assign managers or even executives to walk the floor at one of your locations away from the home office, the information you get can provide a valuable look at your operation.

In fact, this information-gathering process is almost a rite of executive passage for many firms that live and die by the retail dollar. It's not just putting in time behind the counter or at the cash register that these companies require of their managers and executives, but actually having the ability to play the role of the customer. These reports can point to both glaring systems problems and shining examples at the same time.

A noted pediatrician says it even better: "If you want to know what it's like to be a toddler, you have to physically go down to that level. Get down on your hands and knees and crawl around on the floor for a while. You'll see things from a different perspective, and you'll quickly learn what works for you and what doesn't."

CAN YOUR SYSTEMS WALK THE TALK?

➤ *How about some examples of how to evaluate my service systems in action?*

In the following six systems scenarios, look for parallels within your own organization. Even if you're not in the same business or you do different things for your customers, the lessons are the same: Your systems should enable you and your front-line employees to solve customer problems, meet customers needs, and exceed customer expectations.

How would the people and systems in your organization handle the following questions?

The customer wants to return a product

Is this a relatively painless process, or is it long, laborious, or maddening for the customer? Have you created service systems that say, "We'll take your product returns right over here! We'll have plenty of salespeople on duty so you won't have to wait too long. We'll even send a salesperson out into the store, stockroom, or factory to get your replacement product. That way you won't have to search forever or wait forever. We want you to have confidence in this process and know that if you ever have a problem with a product, you shouldn't worry about needing to return it"?

The customer wants a cash refund

Is this even possible with your company? Have you authorized your front-line service people to give cash refunds when necessary (within the guidelines of careful accounting procedures, safe cash handling, and similar security precautions)? If your customer wants a legitimate cash refund, you should have the systems in place to provide it. "We can handle this quickly and efficiently. We promise to have managers or supervisors nearby to authorize cash transactions so you won't have to wait forever for someone to answer a page. We'll give you an immediate cash or credit refund so you won't have to wait six to eight weeks while our headquarters office processes a claim form and sends you a check. It's *our* responsibility to handle the refund and product return process for you."

The customer wants to return something by mail

The Federal Trade Commission, Better Business Bureaus around the country, and even federal, state, and local prosecutors have file cabinets full of complaints from customers who have not been able to exchange their mail-order products. The collection of dull service moments and failed moments of truth surrounding the subject of mail-order products is well known. The fact that many mail-order firms are also small businesses can paint legitimate, hard-working, customer-oriented firms with the same guilty brush.

While some companies do a great job getting you their products, they have no means (read that as no effective system) to help you return the product should you want to. The better firms offer explicit instructions, free postage, or even a reusable mailer to help this process. Companies that have given this real possibility no thought force the customer to waste an afternoon searching for a box, labels, and tape.

The customer wants an answer to a simple question over the telephone

The phrase "Somebody just put me on 'terminal hold'" should not be construed as an endearing one. Of all the external customer-contact systems in use in business, there are few with which we experience more problems than with the telephones. (For all the fluctuations in service, or price, at least your U.S. Postal Service's letter carrier comes by once a day.) Customer feedback about poor telephone systems ranges from "irritated" to "livid."

As you look at the telephone systems and telephone procedures in your own company, are you satisfied with them? Do your people have good telephone skills, including more than basic courtesy, friendliness, and a sensitivity to the time and needs of the customer on the other end?

Passing the customer from one person to another or, worse, from one department to another (so that he or she must explain the question or problem over and over and over) is a sure path to bad marks on the customer's report card. Your telephone systems should be state-of-the-art, but with a human touch added as well. Rather than forcing a customer to park in hold limbo, institute a policy that says, "If we can't answer your question or solve your problem in a short period of your time while on your dime, we'll call you right back on ours."

The customer wants to reach a manager, supervisor, or employee in person or over the phone

Same systems problem, different part of the company. Here, the customer wants to talk to a human being in the company about some issue. With secretaries, front-line service people, and other "gatekeepers" in place to run interference and create roadblocks, the customer can come to feel that he or she is getting a runaround, getting the silent treatment, or being made to feel insignificant.

As you look at your organization, is it easy or even possible for legitimate customers to speak with the people who can help them? The only thing worse than getting the royal runaround on the phone is getting it in person; at least you can hang up the phone.

The customer wants an answer to a complaint letter

It seems to go against our nature to solicit negative feedback, criticisms, or complaints. Yet it's a fact of life that just as there are customers who love us, there are those who wish—to put it gently—we would go climb a tree. The complaint (and resolution) process is a very important part of the service recovery concept and a critical service system in its own right. You have to be ready, willing, and able to take the occasional spoonful of cod liver oil that comes from the unhappy customer. If this means penning a personal response to his or her letter of complaint, so be it.

Of course, you could always follow the example set by George Pullman, of the Pullman Railroad Sleeping Car fame. After receiving a letter from an irate passenger who complained of bedbugs in his berth, Pullman sent the man a very polite, apologetic letter stating that this was the first he had ever heard of such a terrible problem, and that he was taking immediate steps to have the situation rectified. In fact, he was ordering that every Pullman sleeper in operation be pulled off and carefully fumigated before being returned to service.

Unfortunately, he sent back the man's original letter with his response. Written neatly at the bottom was Pullman's note to his secretary, "Send this S.O.B. the 'bedbug' letter."

So much for the spirit of service recovery!

You've probably noticed by now that when you have good service systems in action, it's what the *customer* wants rather than what *you* want. But that's just fine, because by making it easier for your customers to do business with you, you also make it easier for you and your people to do business with them.

If you orient your people around the procedures that help them help their customers, you'll have truly customer-friendly and employee-friendly systems in your small business. That's an advantage not even the big guys can boast about.

LOYALTY VIA DAZZLING SERVICE SYSTEMS: THE BEST COMBINATION

Good service systems are all about doing the right things the right ways. Here's an example of a supermarket that does more than just cut prices, offer double coupons, or recycle your plastic shopping bags. This store doesn't just meet customers' needs, it exceeds their expectations by a factor of ten.

Gelson's, a high-end grocery store that caters to the Los Angeles professional/movie crowd, is famous for its legendary service and out-of-the-ordinary foods.

This California market was first opened in 1949 by two brothers from Iowa, and today it has eight locations that feature everything from edible flowers to \$20/lb. poached salmon. Customers marvel at the spotless store floors, the shopping carts with smooth wheels, the perfectly stocked, label-faced soup cans, and the always-fresh produce. The stack of apples in the fruit area shows an amazing attention to detail: All of the stems face in the same direction!

As one Los Angeles magazine columnist puts it, "Gelson's is renowned for personal service that goes way beyond routinely cooking holiday dinners, catering parties on a day's notice, and putting together elaborate gift baskets for pets."

When heavy winter rains caused winter power outages, store employees followed their customers around with flashlights so that they could still shop in the dark. Following the 1993 Northridge earthquake that caused damage throughout Los Angeles, store employees sold earthquake supplies in the parking lot, even though the market itself was closed.

Signs in the store speak of the store's commitment to its customers: *"Of course, we can specially cut and package meat,"* and *"Of course, we'll help you to your car."*

Since its inception, Gelson's cashiers have not required identification when a customer writes a check, even if that person is not a regular, and this is still the case today. Founder Bernie Gelson puts it this way,

> I [started] a policy of not asking anyone for identification. We felt people's dignity was so important. We made customers that way.[2]

When was the last time you heard of such service at a food store? Even at their best, many of the large national chains are "churn 'em and bag 'em up" operations that offer low prices but little in the way of any additional added value service.

An old joke illustrates the problem at most supermarkets (and other service businesses, for that matter):

A man walked over to the produce clerk with a large head of lettuce in his hand. He said to the clerk, "Excuse me, I can't eat this much lettuce. Would it be possible for you to cut this in half?"

The produce clerk sighed wearily, took the lettuce from the man, and trudged off to the butcher's counter across the store. "Hey, Frank!" he yelled to the butcher in the back room, "Some idiot wants half a head of lettuce!"

At that moment, the produce clerk turned a bit to see the man standing at his elbow. Recovering, he continued, "And this nice gentleman wants the other half!"

A good example of service recovery? I suppose it really depends on whether you're the customer or the grocery store employee.

BUILDING CUSTOMER LOYALTY: USING GOOD SERVICE SYSTEMS TO CREATE REPEAT BUSINESS

Losing or gaining customers can be quite expensive. Studies abound that give all kinds of figures about how much it costs in terms of marketing, advertising, and sales support to get one customer. These figures vary from industry to industry. It may be one thing for a computer hardware manufacturer or lumber mill and quite another for a hardware store chain or convenience store. It doesn't really matter how much it is; suffice it to say that it's not cheap, and it's not likely to go down any time soon.

As I have stated in past pages in this text, it's not what's important to *you* that matters, it's what's important to the *customer*. In few places do we see this stretched to the extreme than in what can be called "upside-down" service systems.

Here, some misguided organizations say, "We have a business to run. We have things to do that the customer never sees. We have goods and services to get out the door in a timely manner. We have to have efficient methods for doing these things. So it's not what's convenient for our customers, it's what's convenient for *us*."

These firms seem to believe that they are in business to serve their own needs, not the customers'. "Hey," goes this reasoning, "if a little pottery gets broken in the process, so be it. We've got to have some control over what we do. Right?"

Wrong. When a customer comes into your store, factory, or office, or otherwise comes into contact with your firm, he or she may need a guided tour through the ins and outs of what it is you do or, more to the point, what you can provide. But here is where upside-down thinking can cause so many problems. The typical "our way or the highway" logic says, "If it's important to us, it must be important to our customers." Again, not true.

Building customer loyalty is a tricky proposition at best. Depending on your existing market share; your location, products, and services, the intensity and number of your competitors; your relative economic strength; and the strength of your existing customer relationships, you can have either with a lot of it or very little.

One small-business owner puts it this way: "Loyalty is important just in terms of the numbers you can generate. If I owned a donut shop, I'd rather sell a dozen donuts a day to 50 of my best, long-time customers than sell one donut at a time to 100 customers over the span of a week."

THE CUSTOMER EVOLUTION: IN WITH THE NEW AND OUT WITH THE OLD?

Reams of material have been written in sales books about how it costs more to get new customers than it does to keep existing ones. This must be a hard lesson to learn because businesspeople don't always seem to abide by its message. In the interest of adding to the fray, here it is again:

Servicing existing customers should be just as important to me, as getting new customers, if not more so.

Look at it this way: "Current customers may know my business, my products and services, my systems, my employees, my methods of operation, and they are in an ideal position to market me and my company to their family, friends, colleagues, and even strangers who may ask them for a referral. New customers are critical to our continuing growth and development, to be sure, but they are new and, by definition, must be taken through our sales process and educated as to what our company can do for them. We want them to become current customers and should work so that this positive cycle of repeat business continues indefinitely."

You get information about the positive and negative parts of your service systems in a variety of ways. Some of it comes from what could be called the intra-ocular test—that is, what hits you between the eyes. Some of it arrives through conversations with your front-line service people or from observations of their duties at the front line with the customer, behind the scenes, or both.

You can gather other information from discussions with the managers and supervisors who guide their people through the various processes of serving and helping the customer. And critical feedback about your systems will come from the customers themselves, who may have very strong opinions in either direction about how easy or hard it is to do business with you.

The customer who flatly says, "I will not be back until you make it easier for me to get my needs met" is not kidding around. If you've discovered systems errors, don't hesitate to change them on demand. It shouldn't take six weeks of memos and meetings to correct a systems problem that the customer faces each time he or she comes into contact with your organization.

And on a more positive side, you also should be able to notice clearly which systems work well and why they do so. It's not always easy to take a hands-off position, even when things couldn't be smoother. If what you've already created serves the customers and your employees well, leave it alone and adjust it only when the need arises.

Of all the important skills you need to own or operate a small business, one of the most powerful ones comes from your commitment to make changes and your willingness to allow them to take root. Good executives and managers have a rare quality known as a tolerance for ambiguity. This trait was best described by Rudyard

Kipling: the ability to "keep your head when all about you are losing theirs."

Taking a thorough look at the core of your small business operations is neither easy nor quick. Making changes in the way you do things takes planning and thought. Don't be shy about asking for help and looking for information from the sources who can steer you to the correct choices.

Notes

1. Milrose B. Basco, "Customer Neglect Called Common Error," San Diego *Union-Tribune*, Oct. 25, 1993, p. C-3.

2. Margo Kaufman, "The Trouble with Gelson's," *BUZZ* magazine, April 1994, 38-39.

Chapter 8

Creating Your Service Surrogate: Selling the Message

"For peace of mind, resign as general manager of the universe."

—LARRY EISENBERG

Most small-business owners and leaders have had to learn the hard way that they cannot be everywhere all the time. For any service quality program to achieve success, the top executive must first believe in the idea and then be able to communicate it to the people who will carry out the plans and continue to spread the word.

The other leaders of the company also must be able to sell the service plan from the top down and then ask other "true believers" to continue to help the front-line employees and nurture their ideas. This chapter is written for you if you're the chief executive of your firm. It will help you to create a winning campaign for your small business service quality program. It includes the people, systems, and attitudes you must surround yourself with in order to have success.

Start by asking this: "What message stays in the room after I leave? If I could eavesdrop on my managers and supervisors, what would they say? How about my front-line service people? Would it be, 'That SOB has another outlandish scheme that won't work' or more like, 'This sounds like a great plan, and we're ready to put it into operation'? Support is not easy to get, but it's crucial. You have to be able to sell your service ideas down the line.

THE CEO AS A WALKING LOGO

One thing that marks any successful service-quality program, in large companies or small businesses, is a dynamic leader. If you look at any well-run company, the chief executive at the top has taken a public stance and said, "This is important. We will run our business to meet the needs of our customers, and I will spend my time making sure our people have the resources and training to do it right."

Bill Marriott, the man whose family name appears on the hotels he runs, is known companywide for his commitment to his service-minded employees. He travels several weeks each month to his many hotel, kitchen, and food-service properties. When he arrives, he makes it a point to shake the hand of every employee in the building.

This handshake is not just reserved for the hotel manager, the head of the kitchen operations, or the airline food services chief; *everyone* who is on the job at the time he comes to call. Maids, desk clerks, janitors, chefs, bell staff, telephone operators, cooks— it doesn't matter who, Marriott meets them all.

"Some people may think that's a bit corny," says Marriott, "but I take it very seriously. I think it's important for our people to know I'm committed to their work."

Marriott, who must know what it feels like to be a presidential candidate "working the crowd," wants to serve as a walking, talking symbol of the customer-first attitude that permeates the Marriott conglomerate. He relishes his role as the "point man" for the company. He wants everyone who works for him to be able to say, "I met Bill Marriott, the man whose name is on the building, and he has seen what I do here."

And Marriott is not a pioneer in this sense of carrying the company message. Former Chrysler chief Lee Iacocca started something with his appearances as the TV and radio spokesman for his car company, and other CEOs have followed suit. When you see Wendy's chief Dave Thomas, Carl's Jr. CEO emeritus Carl Karcher, and Disney's Michael Eisner on TV commercials, it's for more reasons than just executive ego.

These men have taken on the role of identifying themselves with their products. While customers may come to know them through the commercials or other public appearances, the *employees* recognize that their leader has taken a public position about the company, its products, and its people. Say what you will about Iacocca's management style, when he went on the air and said, "We're making a better car and we're leading the world in minivans," people—customers, Chrysler employees, and Chrysler competitors—believed him.

While it's not necessary for you to go on TV and pitch your products or services, if you're the CEO, it behooves you to take on a high-profile role in your company as the spokesperson for your employees and your customers.

The extent of your role depends upon a number of factors:

- Your time commitments for your own daily decision making.

- Your travel schedule and the number and distances of other company work sites.

- The strength and depth of your chain of command—who can run the operations while you are out of the office for short or long periods of time.

- Your comfort level with making speeches, appearing in front of groups of your employees, or opening each service-quality training session or seminar with remarks and encouragement.

- Your ability to be frequently visible as both a company leader and a *manager* of strategies, systems, and people.

- Your ability to tell your managers and supervisors, "This service-quality program and these ideas are important to me and important to the success of this company. I expect you to get behind me and help the program survive and thrive."

- Your commitment to telling your employees, "This is what will guide us from now on. I'm behind these ideas, your managers and supervisors are behind them, and I want you to believe in them as well. We will give you the tools, training, and opportunity to make them work for you. We encourage your feedback, and we promise to act on your suggestions when we can."

- Your ability to delegate responsibilities to those who can free your time to concentrate more on your "spokesperson" role. The only thing worse than *undercommitting* yourself, your company, and your resources to a service-quality program is *overcommitting* yourself so that you try to do too much and therefore get very little done.

- Your desire to respond to customer complaints, positive and negative feedback, and suggestions, as well as all feedback, suggestions, and ideas from your employees at all levels. Flexibility and humility are missing commodities in many unsuccessful leaders; good ones know how to change on demand when the data points to the need.

- Your ability to "suffer the slings and arrows of outrageous fortune" and stick to your program even through the rocky times. Any commitment to a service program will have its up and down days as your management team, your employees, and your customers get used to new ideas, new systems, and new ways to help each other along.

- Finally, your understanding of three related key concepts: *service planning, service direction*, and *service leadership*. In effect, these three ideas cover the beginning, middle, and ongoing phases of any service quality program.

    In terms of planning, you've got to discover what's

important to your customers, then be ready to turn your organization around to give it to them. This may mean a new strategy, new systems, and new plans.

In terms of direction, you've got to preach the message to your executives, train your managers and supervisors to make your plans operational, and tell your employees what to expect.

In terms of leadership, you must be ready to serve as the "lighthouse" for your entire organization.

A MODEL OF YOUR SERVICE CHAMPIONS

Any movement toward a service quality program should start with *service planning*. You, your top executives, and your managers should meet on a frequent basis to discuss ideas, create plans, and focus on the nuts-and-bolts operational items that pertain to your specific business, industry, and market.

➤ *What are some of the elements of this service planning?*

This is where the hard questions get asked: "What business are we *really* in?" "What do our customers tell us they want, in terms of their needs and expectations?" and "How do we orient our service systems to meet the needs of our service providers so that they meet the customers' needs?"

At this point, as the plans, procedures, and operations start to take place, you'll need to assign certain people to certain roles, jobs, and duties. Here's a bold idea: When it comes time to start your service quality program, ask for volunteers from your management staff. If no one puts up a hand, ask why not. If you strongly believe in the program and can't get any backers from your managers, go out and get new managers who will implement your plans!

You must have support and commitment from your management staff. If you don't have it, any service quality program you attempt probably will not make it past six months. If you're surrounded by a roomful of naysayers, disbelievers, and other apathetic, "that-won't-work-here" managers, your organization is probably in more trouble than you know.

Of course, there may be perfectly valid reasons why now is not the time for you to undertake a new service-quality program. You may not have enough operating capital to fund such an effort. You may have significant internal management, product, or employee problems that must be resolved prior to any new effort. Your business may be in transition—through a sale; a buyout; a merger; the acquisition of another company or division; layoffs; plant, office, or store closures; bankruptcy recovery; etc. And finally, you just may not have the management horses to help you pull the plow.

But to be honest, if you expect your firm to be in business for the long haul, you're going to have to make the necessary commitment to a service-quality initiative of some type just to stay competitive. Your customers want their needs met and are looking to have their expectations exceeded. They demand high-end service from you and your people, and they will look elsewhere if they don't get it.

Waiting for the right time to start a service quality program is like waiting for the right time to have children if you're married. If you factor in all the reasons why it might be better to wait, you'll end up with no new offspring, and it will ultimately be too late to change your mind.

There's never an absolutely perfect time to do anything, whether it's having kids, buying real estate, or changing the face and direction of your business. Sometimes you just have to say, "This is the best it's going to get. Waiting will not make things better. It's time to move now."

Once you have your course of action in mind, it's time to form the management team that will help you get where you want to go. In short, you must handpick your service champions—the people who see things the same way you do, believe in the same service philosophy you do ("It's the customer"), and are willing to put themselves and their careers on the line to prove it.

➤ *Should I look for total and complete agreement from my managers or just group consensus?*

It's probably not realistic to think that everyone will be in love with you or your programs. Group consensus says, "While we may not all agree on this course of action, as a whole we think it will work, and we will follow your lead."

This is also not to say that you want to surround yourself with yes-men and women. Such managers will tell you what they think you want to hear, which may or may not be the actual truth. What you want is managers with enough guts to commit to a service-quality program and enough fortitude to come to you with suggestions, feedback, and new ideas to make things work even better.

This last area, in fact, should be one of your requirements: constant feedback from your management staff as to what's working and what's not. You don't want to hear, "I knew there were problems, but I didn't want to come to you with them because I knew how important this program was to you." Your key executives and managers should be able to say, "I've come to you because there are some problems and I know how important his program is to *all of us.*"

Here's a prescription for *service champions*, offering a model of the kinds of people you want running your service programs. It's not meant to describe the "perfect" employee or other unattainable pie-in-the-sky goals. It should just give you an idea of the caliber of executive and management staff you'll want to have around you:

- They buy into the "customer-first" idea and are not still stuck in the old TQM mindset that focuses on manufacturing outputs rather than serving the customer.

- They will not bad-mouth the program, talk derisively about you or any portion of it in public, or otherwise distract from the message that says, "This is important to our growth and development as an organization."

- They have a good grasp of the concepts of service management. They know and understand basic themes like the moments of truth, the elements of the Service Triangle™, the steps in each Cycle of Service, the customer's mental report card, the need for customer- and employee-friendly systems, and the need for customer-oriented front-line employees.

- Individually, they can offer ideas about the service strategy for the company; e.g., "I think our strategy statement should reflect the following key factors . . ." or "Here are the customer value factors that I feel make us superior to our competitors . . ."

- They know their divisions, departments, units, and teams well enough to be able to look at their respective service systems with an objective eye, e.g., "Here's what works in terms of the way we process customer orders, and here's what needs improvement . . ."

- They know the work, the attitudes, and the personalities of each of their front-line service providers. They can see who works well with the customers and who needs improvement. They're willing to talk to their people and provide training, suggestions, and input into the way that they serve their customers, meet their customers' needs, and attempt to exceed their customers' expectations.

- They understand the concept of external and internal customers and realize that they have internal customers of their own. In fact, they see themselves as customers of the front-line people, e.g., "I will do what it takes to give my people the skills, materials, training, supervision, and guidance they need so that they can best devote their energies to serving their customers."

- When called upon, they are willing to teach and preach the service-quality message at all levels of the organization. This includes attending the same training seminars as the front-line employees, meeting with them at the employees' convenience, not theirs, and backing the program's ideas at every stage.

- They are willing to model the service behaviors they expect from their employees. If this means going out to work on the factory floor, getting behind the cash register, or pitching in to answer phones, they do it. No job is beneath them, and they will work hard to prove this to the front-line employees.

- In some capacity, they will spend at least some portion of each month working directly with external customers. This means that they will not sit in their offices behind closed doors, but will roll up their sleeves, go out to the front line, and meet customers face to face to answer questions, handle complaints, or suggest solutions.

- They are willing to gather feedback, reflect upon it, and then act decisively on it. This includes comments from the employees and the customers. They will actively solicit feedback from the customers by creating functional information-gathering systems that make it easy for them to give it. They promise to respond to customer feedback, either by meeting with the customer personally or by discussing the issue with the front-line service provider. They also will create systems to attract and encourage employee feedback and offer a complete report on the change steps they have taken.

- They are willing to take guidance, suggestions, and even criticism from you and their peers about what works and what does not.

- They are willing to report back to you, establish clear lines of communication with your office, and serve as the sounding board for information that comes from the employees on the front line and their customers.

HOW TO CLONE YOURSELF: MAKING YOUR MESSAGE YOUR DEPUTY

➤ *Who will follow my orders, sell my message to the front-line people, and continue to preach my "service gospel" when I leave the room?*

The short answer is "my executives and managers." The longer answer is "my front-line service providers." And in terms of the big picture, the real answer can be "my company as a whole." Let's take a look at each of your respective torch carriers.

Enlisting help to spread your message company wide serves you by telling one and all what's important to you. It also guides those around you, even when you're not around to provide leadership, management skills, motivation, and, just as important, blatant enthusiasm.

As I've described at length in the above section, to have quality people at your executive and managerial levels is not a good idea, it's *critical*. You should hold them to the same high levels of service accountability as you do your front-line people, if not to higher levels.

Once your top folks have been indoctrinated in the ways of the customer, you should feel comfortable about turning them loose on the rest of the members of the organization, armed with the same message: "Go forth and spread the word to everyone here. This is how we will do business from now on. I can't be everywhere, and in some respects I can only serve as a figurehead for this plan. I need your help to implement all the service elements we've designed for our organization."

Management Assistance

Your personal service message should mirror your firm's overall service strategy. Your key people should not have to guess what you believe in or what you want; based on meetings and planning sessions, they should already know. It's their job to take this same message and let it permeate every level of the company.

And your personal service message also can become a part of

the written training materials that your front-line people receive as part of their exposure to your new service-quality program. Many CEOs like to write an open letter to all the employees telling them exactly what will happen in the coming months. Here's an excerpt from one used by the director of a hospital:

> You have an important part to play as we strive to meet our objective of improving the quality of service we provide to our customers. Without you, and without your commitment to do a good job, we would not be able to provide the outstanding level of service our customers demand and should receive.
>
> Part of this new program will involve some training sessions to help you see your jobs in a new and better way. By the end of our training program, we hope you will have a new sense of commitment to our mission of service quality, a new belief in the idea that excellent service is the only kind worth giving, and a new sense of the value of working together with each other as a complete service team.

As you can see, much of this message involves the word "you," and this is no accident. Empowering the front-line service employee is a "you" process, as in, "Here's what we're going to do to help *you* help *your* customers. Here's what we want *you* to do to help us reach the goal of excellence in service." Your support staff should continue to help you "walk the walk and talk the talk" as it pertains to this venture into service excellence. And it's not enough for your staff just to *follow* your orders; they have to be willing to put their own spin of commitment behind your words and calls for action. Your executives and managers should have enough foresight to say to their people, "People, here's what this service program is all about. Now, here's what it means to *you* and *your* job."

Front-Line Assistance

Your front-line service employees can help you spread the service message in a variety of unique ways. For one thing, there are more of those folks than there are managers, so you can strengthen the repetition and volume of your message through their sheer numbers. For another, they are the closest link to each other that you have in the organization. The word from on Management High can take only you so far. For any service-quality program to get off the ground and take flight, you need and must have *employee commitment*.

And much of this commitment is created at the ground level, far from any training workshops, hands-on management, or other company-sponsored events that you officially use to promote service quality. Don't underestimate the power of the grapevine.

> *Are you really talking about gossip and other similar asides?*

Like few other members of your organization, the people who directly serve the customer hear things, see things, and learn things that can have a great impact on the success or health of your program. They always have their ears to the company railroad track, so to speak. They hear the vibrations around them, whether they come from customers, fellow employees, competitors, or even colleagues or associates outside your company. What they say about their participation in your program as they sit in their break rooms or at the water cooler or coffee pot can serve as an accurate measure of how things are going.

One veteran seminar leader I know says, "If you want to find out what they *really* think about you or your training program, just be the first one into the bathroom at the first coffee break. You'd be amazed at what they'll say and what you can hear about your training techniques from a nearby stall!"

Seriously, what you or your managers may shrug off as gossip or idle chat may actually be closer to the truth than you realize. Don't hesitate to include this kind of bottom-line feedback in your assessment of any ongoing program, training, or service systems changes.

Finally, your front-line service employees are also your closest link *to the customer*. People talk, and customers and employees can develop relationships and even friendships over time. As you can guess, not all of their daily conversation is strictly on business—"Here's what I want" and "Okay, here it is." Your employees will often take their valued customers into their trusted confidence to discuss major changes going on around them. And like it or not, these conversations create impressions in your customers' minds about how you conduct business.

Obviously, if your front-line people feel more empowered by a new service-quality initiative, if they feel that they are actually part of the decision-making process, and if they feel that these changes are largely for the better, they will give your program glowing marks.

Of course, the converse is also true, and while you can't stop a few disgruntled people from poor-mouthing parts of the program that they don't like or agree with, it makes no sense to allow widespread bad feelings to permeate and ruin good customer relationships. As we will see in the next chapter on how to keep your program up and running strong, "bad apple" management can be an important task for your managers and supervisors.

So what do you do to prevent these kinds of employee-customer exchanges? Nothing! They are a legitimate and normal part of any significant business exchange. This is not to say that these kinds of conversations are going on every minute, but you probably can surmise when and where they are taking place between your people and their customers.

To back up a bit, if you can't stop 'em, join 'em. Why not *encourage* your front-line employees to talk up your new service quality program? Why not let them be your ambassadors of change and goodwill? What's wrong with telling them, "It's okay to talk about what we're doing with your customers. They may be encouraged to see that we're trying to make changes for the better, thereby creating a better service experience for them, too. And they may have their own thoughts, feedback, suggestions, and even complaints. That's okay, because we'll take all of the information we can get, from you and from them."

Remember, the way your employees feel about your organization is how they will feel when they talk to your customers.

➤ *Service really is all about people, isn't it?*

In a word, yes, which is why you should always strive to surround yourself with the sharpest possible people—from the top down and from the bottom up. And don't forget that it takes just as much effort from the front-line people as it does from the "suits." Companies have slipped badly because they failed to account for the needs of the people who do the "real" work with the customer each day. You need to exercise just as much care in choosing the people who serve the customer as you do when you appoint the people who work directly for you.

My Company 'Tis of Me

Finally, you should always let your company sell your service message as well. Follow this line of thinking for a moment.

➤ *What do my customers see all the time that makes them think of us?*

Your delivery trucks, your packaging, your products, your logo, the uniforms your people wear, your letterhead and business cards, your catalogs, your giveaway items or gifts, posters, bumper stickers, billboards along the freeway, direct-mail pieces, or advertising? Why not include some or all of your service message in these things?

As your employees sell products, have them give the customer a small card with your service strategy printed on it. Have them include some literature about the customer benefits of your service-quality initiative in the next mail-order shipment. Drop them a short note that begins, "An Open Letter to Our Customers."

McDonald's and Jack in the Box use tray placemat liners to advertise new products or to talk about their commitment to service quality. Think about what you can use to spread your service quality message to your current and *new* customers. Be creative; think outside the lines of what you would normally do.

In today's competitive marketplace, catchy sells. A look at any recent TV commercial or full-page magazine ad will reaffirm that for you. Put your collective management heads together, or hire an ad agency or a public relations firm and give it an assignment: "Publicize our commitment to service quality in such a way as to make it memorable."

Word of mouth, referrals, and targeted "service marketing" pieces can bring you a surprising amount of new business. Don't just advertise your company, advertise your service message as well. It's not just your products or services that interest the customer, it's the way he or she is served that makes the difference. If that were not true, instead of grocery stores, we would all buy our food in giant, dimly lit warehouses where all of the packages looked the same; instead of shopping at a dealership, we would all buy our cars out of the same catalog; and instead of a nice restaurant, we would all eat the same food in the same cafeteria-style rooms.

It is the sizzle as well as the steak that sells things for us. Use new and creative means to tell your customers—current ones or prospects—"Something good *for you* is going on around here!"

PERSONNEL RESPONSIBILITIES: LINKING THE CHAIN OF COMMAND

As we have discussed, for any service-quality program to fly, you've got to have continuing support throughout the organization. This brings us to a discussion of the ebb and flow of people, personnel, and power in your small business. Different people have different agendas. Some of them are quite visible, and others are more hidden, or even devious. How and where you muster support for your programs, by working through or around these agendas, is another sink-or-swim issue. Even if you own the joint, it helps to start thinking about the collections of power and influence around you. As songster Bob Dylan so aptly put it, "It may be the Devil or it may be the Lord, but you're gonna have to serve somebody."

If you're already the CEO or owner, do you report to a board of directors, stockholders, your parent company, your franchiser, your partners, or your venture capitalists? It's always wise to include these people (and their agendas, known or otherwise) in your thinking and planning about any new service program. While you may not have to walk them all through every stage, it's nice to have additional support and other allies, and you can at least hope that these people will be able to talk knowledgeably about what it is you're trying to do. Sometimes their input and feedback can be quite valuable, since they see things from a different perspective than you might.

Even if you own or operate your firm and command all you can see from the top seat, who are you personally responsible to? What is the chain of command above or below you? And what do you need to tell these people or groups about any service program you undertake? Depending upon their needs or the health, type, or history of your relationship with them, you might tell them everything so that they will take a complete hands-on role while you supervise the process, or you might run most of the program yourself and give them highly specific duties.

Much of this depends upon your management style. Some owners are more hands-on, and others are more hands-off. You need to be able to strike a balance that says, "Here is the program and here are your duties and responsibilities," then decide how much day-to-day input you want to impart.

If you'll recall the discussion in Chapter 2 about the service and business turnaround created at SAS, Jan Carlzon had a real "participatory" style of management. He so believed in the strength of service management concepts that he even had a computer installed in his office to track the on-time rates of his firm's flights. It was not uncommon for extra-tardy pilots to get a computer memo from CEO Carlzon asking why their flight was delayed.

CREATE A SERVICE MANAGEMENT SWAT TEAM

The idea here is the same as the one I discussed in Chapter 6 when I suggested the creation of a roving employee-led service SWAT team. And while that group should focus on issues related to the health and happiness of both their front-line coworkers and their customers, the management team can deal with leadership and supervision issues. Plus, there is still room for crossover duties that relate to serving customers as well by solving problems, mediating complaints, and making decisions that the front-line employee may not have the power to do.

Your management SWAT team doesn't have to be large in size, just in thinking and activity. Even if it consists of only two highly-motivated leaders, it can serve as an effective go-between for your office and the front-line people.

➤ *How do I get the people to come on board?*

You may want to staff this team with one department head from each division or one manager from each department (to allow the department head to stay in charge of his or her unit); you could ask for volunteers from your managers; or you could ask your department heads to select the people themselves.

Membership on this team should be strictly voluntary and not seen as punishment. What you want is people who can think, lead, manage, and communicate with the front-line people, with their customers, and, ultimately, with you.

Just as the front-line employees often have the best ideas about how to serve the customer, your managers often know what works best and who works best at the front-line. Your service management SWAT team should be able to roam the organization at will, observing systems and people at work, watching the many customer interactions that take place each day, classifying the many moments of truth they see, observing the Cycle of Service at work; and generating and collecting feedback from other managers, front-line employees, and customers.

Your goal with any service initiative is to encourage parallel movement toward and for your message, and not allow unnecessary competition among departments, managers, supervisors, or employees that will dilute, distract, dissuade, or destroy it.

This is especially difficult if you have an aggressive sales force or a sales force that works strictly on commission. Salespeople may take their eyes off the ball in their attempt to win customers and commissions for themselves. The overall goal should be success as a team, not just as an individual. As the old coaches always say, "There is no *I* in 'team.'"

If you see these kinds of problems where your people are being customer-competitive for all the wrong reasons, it may be time to step in with some systems changes, including the way people are compensated or rewarded for their actions.

TECHNOLOGY IS OUR FRIEND

It's time for a news flash: Be ready to integrate new technology to make your systems accessible to you, your accountants, plant foremen, builders, designers, bookkeepers, inventory controllers, and any other group of your people who need to run them. The days of keeping your business affairs in your head are long over. The term "small business" doesn't mean that your data is not complex enough to require a hard and fast move into the realm of high-tech.

This is the Information Age—in fact, it's going to be the Super Information Age. As we speed through the 1990s en route to the fabled year 2000, it's plain to see that the computer is here to stay. By now, even the worst "technophobe" among us has come to the conclusion that he or she must have at least a budding familiarity with the "green-glowing box of microchips" known as the personal computer (PC).

Some firms have made the inevitable switch to computerized systems with hardly a sigh. Others have had to drag their CEOs, executives, managers, and other employees kicking and screaming into the future.

A story in a recent business magazine illustrates this. It seems that one of Wal-Mart's smaller competitors (which describes most of them) was faced with some important decisions about replacing its outdated electronic cash registers.

Over at Wal-Mart, the computer systems that serve as cash registers keep a careful tally of each store's inventory. If a customer buys a garden hose, the computer notes the item number in the inventory, cross checks it with the stock on hand, and, if more stock is needed, automatically places an order for garden hoses with Wal-Mart's distribution center.

At the competitor, when someone buys that same garden hose, the electronic cash register rings up the price, spits out a receipt, calculates the change for the customer, and ends the transaction.

The difference is like apples and oranges. At Wal-Mart, high tech has made for better inventory control, no empty store shelves, and customers who will say, "Boy, there sure are a lot of garden hoses to choose from here."

At the competitor, you have no additional data other than the time, date, and price of the transaction. Inventory control is still tallied by hand—store employees must go out on to the sales floor and count the garden hoses one by one.

While this is just a small example, it does point out the need for your small business to keep up the pace. Whether it's computers; optical scanners; color printing technology; computer ID cards that track products, people, and services; CD-ROM technology; CAD-CAM design systems; computer-based accounting, personnel, or payroll management; or any other electronic, high-tech, or time-and-effort-saving gizmo or system, you need to stay competitive by embracing high technology.

▶ *But I don't like computers. I still don't have one on my desk. What's wrong with pen-and-paper systems?*

For all their faults, computers are still designed to make our working lives easier, and for the most part, they do. Take payroll services, for example. What used to take hours or even days to compute by hand—FICA rates, unemployment insurance, state and federal taxes, etc.—now requires just a few taps of the computer keyboard; checks, stubs, and all the required data are produced automatically.

And handy financial information—P&L statements, income and balance sheet reports, expense reports, etc.—is now right at your fingertips. Nearly anything you want to write, calculate, observe, or discuss is now on a computer somewhere. With rapid changes in hardware and software technology, you can build computer systems that can run your entire small business for under $15,000.

If you're still a technophobe, hire an outside computer consultant or draft someone knowledgeable from your organization and tell him or her to train you and any other key person on your staff who needs to be computer-literate.

These days, not knowing anything about computers is certainly nothing to boast about. In some cases, it can be a liability for your company. If you're still not convinced that your small business can benefit from more widespread computer use, consider the following advantages:

- *Speed.* You can get instant updates on the status of orders at the touch of a button. Most software programs allow you to keep track of individual orders by entering the customer's name. In seconds, the entire electronic file appears, giving dates, prices, and deadlines. With this system in place, you can get an entire sales history right on the screen.

- *Accuracy.* While it's not true that computers never make mistakes, the structure of many database management programs won't allow you to enter improper data or make many mistakes. Storing customer information on computers forces you to follow careful data entry procedures. This is a powerful asset, when combined with good computer-use habits, such as finishing each entry task in order, updating the orders when necessary, and protecting the computer from harm just as if it were a living member of the office staff.

- *Safety.* With the prudent use of all-important backup floppy disks and hard disk tape drive backup systems, and careful handling of the software and hardware, the computer can work for years and years without failure. Some small businesses lock their computerized files (the backup disks or tapes themselves) in a sturdy safe at the end of each business day. This protects the files—truly the life-blood of any organization—from fire, water damage, or theft.

- *Confidentiality.* Standard filing cabinets don't offer much security from theft or sabotage for paper files, nor do they keep prying eyes away. Some software programs offer "encryption" anti-hacker protection, meaning that if you don't enter the proper password, employee ID number, or, literally, the correct key for the lockable keyhole, you don't get in. This protects the files from accidental or deliberate erasure and from any other electronic eavesdropping that might take place.

Given the wide range of computer software programs available that are designed specifically for the needs of companies like yours, it just makes good sense to take advantage of the powers offered by a personal computer.

Rules of Change to Help Your Service Quality Program

Like using computers, everything you do as a company leader should benefit the customer in some way. While this sounds like a broad stroke of the brush, consider the facts:

Every system you create that helps your front-line people also helps their customers, at least indirectly. Every policy you create that improves the way your managers manage or your front-line employees serve helps their internal and external customers. And the training and support you give to your front-line employees to empower them to act as the customer's agent for change helps the customer.

For all of these good things, it's also easy to get carried away or lose sight of what works and what doesn't. In small-business operations, you've got to think smarter, faster, and more often than the big guys do. Thanks to your size and balance sheet data, you can't toss a few million bucks into one failed program after another. Your programs have to work right the first time. Keep these things in mind as you go:

1. *Start slowly and plan, plan, plan.* The time for planning is in the beginning, not once you're underway. When NASA sends a spacecraft to land on Mars, it doesn't aim it for where Mars is now; it aims it for where Mars is going to be when the ship *gets there.* Course adjustments in midflight are fine and even necessary, just don't start off without knowing the direction you want to take.

2. *Look before you leap.* The person who once said, "All change is good" never owned or operated a small business. Aggressive movements are always commendable, provided they fix what's broken or improve upon something that already works. Even if you're in charge and the buck stops at your desk, it never hurts to talk to the people around you. They may give you the one missing piece or bright idea you've needed all along.

3. *Start with complete scans of the Service Triangle™, write and rewrite your service strategy, look hard at your systems for service delivery, and then look at your service providers and their managers and supervisors.* Enough said.

4. *Get feedback before you make changes or improvements that may only sound good to you or look great on paper.* Ditto.

5. *What you do, in terms of instigating changes, will affect everyone, including employees, systems, and customers that you might not have seen or considered.* Changing systems is just like tinkering with plumbing pipes. Each time you tighten one thing, another one leaks, and each time you reroute a pipe from one area to another, the water pressure changes. One system affects another, which affects another, and so on. Keep the big picture in mind.

6. *Make adjustments to the company carburetor first; don't try to overhaul the organization's engine in one day.* As a small business, you must crawl before you walk and walk before you run. You can do only so much, and a lot of what you can accomplish depends upon the people and operations that are already in place. Start by looking at the critical moments of truth for your business and your customers and tackle them first.

7. *Whether you are or aren't at the top, get or emphasize senior management support at the start of any service initiative.* You have to have it in order to succeed. Educate your colleagues, make converts, and encourage them to look at the organization as you have and come up with ideas of their own.

8. *Don't change for the sake of change—no churn management strategies that just create stress in your employees and customers and end up crashing and burning later anyway.* Okay?

9. *Do the right things the right way with the right people.* The old saying, "There's always time to do it right the first time" fits here. It's not always more money or new materials or new equipment that makes things work better; small-business success still starts and ends with good people at all levels of the organization.

10. *Use the customer as your "artificial horizon" and center of gravity.* Does this change help or hinder our customers? Reflect our service strategy? Improve our service systems? Assist and aid our employees to meet the customers' needs and exceed their expectations? Make your decisions with your customers in mind, now and forever.

How to Make Change When You Don't Own the Bank

➤ *Okay, I'm committed to making the right choices about service to the customer. But what if I'm **not** the owner or operator of my company? How can I make my firm different when I don't call all of the shots?*

As you can imagine if you're in this position, this is a common query. You can have the brightest ideas in the world, but if you're not in a position of either power or influence or both, it can make for tough sledding. Unread reports, mishandled suggestions, apathy, ignorance, or any of the other seven hundred deadly sins can go a long way toward quashing your initial enthusiasm.

In small businesses, there may be a very tight circle of leadership. It may include one person—the owner or CEO—or a small cadre of ranking executives. In any case, selling your ideas about service to them will be just like selling a product to a customer. You'll have to explain the obvious and hidden benefits, make them understand the facts and figures, and show why it makes sense to do something now.

In many ways, it helps to have some friends in the room. Many up-and-coming executives have mentor/coach relationships with certain key people above them who can provide information, influence, and support. If you haven't developed this kind of relationship in your organization, find someone whose management style you admire and ask for help. This makes your introduction into the CEO's office that much easier, and when it comes time to put your plans on the table for open inspection, you already have some built-in allies.

Here are some other ideas to help you sell yourself and your ideas upstairs:

- *Manage your own fiefdom well first.* Stay out of turf wars, personality clashes, and other career stoppers. Become known for good management skills and better people skills. Let your results speak for you when you're not there.

- *Lead by example.* Most front-line service people would like to see the boss get his or her hands dirty once in a while. If you're not willing to do something—an unpleasant task, a dirty job, dealing with an irate customer, etc.— you shouldn't have the right to ask your people to do it either.

- *Hire a strong group of service providers.* Good employees can make you look like a winner, and bad ones can make you look as if you or your area is totally out of control. If you have any input into the hiring process, now's the time to use it.

- *Model the behavior you want in your people.* If you want good customer contacts, show them how it's done. Explain the moments of truth concepts and tell them where they fit into it. If you're committed to any service quality program, you've got to be ready to walk the talk.

- *Create a specific service strategy and service systems for the employees under your control.* Even if you can't control all of the systems, you can make the ones that directly involve you or your people the best they can be. Strive for a reputation that says, "Those folks over in that department are really on the ball."

- *Meet with top management and be prepared to point to hard numbers, key result areas, and success stories.* Many top executives have a numbers background. For the ones who were born and weaned on hard financial data, you'd better have your spreadsheets in a row. If you can say the magic words, "Here's what we're *spending* now to attract each customer and here's what we can *save* by putting this plan into operation," you'll win more of the converts you need. And an occasional shining star service story or moment thrown in for good measure can't help but sway the crowd at the top.

- *Offer a plan that sounds like it came from the top anyway.* In some cases you have to be ready to say, "Who cares who gets the glory? As long as they know it came from me."

- *Ask for the chance to run with the ball.* If you've designed and built a feasible service quality program, ask for permission to take it to the troops and send it company-wide.

- *Be ready to accept the challenges, blame, and problems that go with this new territory.* And if you do get the chance to run the program, toughen up your hide and forge ahead.

- *Establish lines of communication that go straight to the top.* The top brass probably will build this into any marching plan they give you. If not, give them regular reports on your progress, setbacks, needs, and achievements.

- *Make continuous service improvements in the areas you do control.* If you're responsible for one or more departments, make them the best ones in your organization. Focus on what you can control, and leave what you can't to others.

Fear not; even if you aren't in total control of the organization, you can still *influence* those who are. Some of the best service management programs in existence came from the middle management ranks first. The people in the company who are responsible for the training, staff development, employee education, human resources, customer service, and customer quality control areas have often used their own initiative to design winning service-quality programs that received the seal of approval from the CEO's office.

Chapter 9

Ten Critical Success Factors: Doing the Right Things with the Right People

"When you aim for perfection, you discover it's a moving target."

—GEORGE FISHER

Now that you understand how to implement a service program, this chapter offers you more advice on keeping it up and running. Heeding these ten success factors can mean the difference between being a marginal small-business service company that can't keep customers and being an outstanding service firm that attracts them in droves.

As the TV and print media have aptly demonstrated, with several of their favorite topics, it's always easier to bash things as bad then to promote them as good. This chapter will offer you a positive message and focus on the upside of your small business. In effect, here's how to keep the flywheel of your company's service quality program spinning.

1. SELECT THE BEST SERVICE PEOPLE

If you look at employment at your company as a river, your new employees will jump into the water at the beginning and ride along until they reach the end of the river and—theoretically—retire. As they go along, either they demonstrate certain skills, qualities, and personality traits that make them suitable for the jobs you give them or they don't.

With bad, useless, destructive, or lazy employees, these negative traits appear fairly quickly—maybe not within the first week, but possibly within the first six weeks, and by the end of six months for sure. Many of the problem behaviors they exhibit— bad attitudes with their customers, inability to get along well with coworkers, insubordination toward their managers and supervisors, etc.—may in fact have shown up during the interview and hiring process. So what happened? Somebody, either you or the person doing the hiring, forgot, neglected, or just didn't look at the warning signs.

Hiring good people, the ones who can provide the best service to your customers, is like standing at the source of a river. What you put into the water will always end up downstream. So why not, to continue the metaphor, put the best people in the water at the start?

One of the tried and true messages we've learned from our personnel experts is, "It's always easier to hire good people at the start than it is to get rid of bad ones later." Yet, for some reason, some owners and HRD or personnel types fail to notice the warning signs when they hire people to staff important front-line service roles in their small businesses.

In a 1994 case of workplace violence in Tulsa, Oklahoma, a man employed by the Wendy's hamburger chain was asked by his boss to come in early and help out. Apparently, this request went against his way of thinking, for he showed up at the fast-food restaurant armed with a handgun. When he was finished venting his rage, six people had been shot and wounded. Thankfully, through some miracle of modern medicine, none of them died.

Tulsa police and Wendy's company officials looking into this case discovered that the man had been let go from several other fast-food restaurants in the area, including other Wendy's establishments. Because he had exhibited some behavioral problems, he was given a "not recommended for rehire" reference in his Wendy's employment file.

Through some gross act of mismanagement or error, his employment file was misplaced at the local Wendy's headquarters, and he managed to get hired again by another unsuspecting franchisee.

While the phrase "These things happen" is small consolation for the wounded and their families, the eyewitnesses, the bystanders, and the other Wendy's employees, it does make a point. These things *do* happen. Now more than ever, you must exercise great care about whom you hire. And since your front-line people are in direct contact with the lifeblood of your company, the customers, it's important that you choose the right folks for the right jobs.

The applicant who left his last three jobs because he "didn't get along with his bosses" should raise a red flag. The applicant who says, "I don't really like dealing with customers and all their problems, but I need a job," should not be your first or fiftieth front-line service choice. And the applicant who says, "How much am I gonna be paid?" before he or she asks, "What are my job duties?" probably will not last too long either.

So what do you do to hire the best service employees you can find? Ask for help from the people who *already* work for you.

The old adage "It's not what you do but who you know" certainly applies in job hunting. During your own job-hunting days, you probably found that a kind referral from friends who worked at companies that interested you meant the difference between having your resume sandwiched in a pile with 300 others and getting an interview with the personnel manager.

So if networking worked for you as an individual, why not try it in reverse? When a new position opens, ask your employees to help you fill it.

"We've found that the best way to get good people who agree with our mission statement and core values and are compatible with the way we work is to network," says a VP of human resources for a high-tech engineering firm.

He says that whenever the firm has an open position, it asks its employees to spread the word among friends, colleagues, and peers. "We recruit by networking first, especially at the executive and managerial levels."

It's easier to find qualified people through networking than with ads in the newspaper. Further, when your employees recruit new people, they can often vouch for them on many different levels, such as education, background, work experience, and just how well they get along with others, including customers, if they've worked with them in other service jobs.

To hire the right people, you'll need to interview carefully, check references, and do a background check as well. And this goes just as much for executive and managerial applicants as it does for front-line service people and their behind-the-scenes counterparts. Plenty of unsuspecting personnel managers have been snowed by inflated resumes coming from people applying for high-level positions.

Check and recheck whoever you plan to hire; you're going to have to live with each other for some time, and it helps to feel comfortable with your decision. Review some of the hiring criteria in Chapter 6, and don't discount your gut instincts. See if you can answer yes to the following questions, "Will this person fit in with our service goals, strategy, and systems? Will he or she work hard to meet our customers' needs and exceed their expectations? Do I feel comfortable bringing this person into our small-business family?"

2. GET THEM STARTED IN THE RIGHT DIRECTION

It often helps to think of your employees as your customers. At some time during the buying process, all customers need some support, guidance, and maybe even some training. And so it goes with your front-line service employees. Nobody was born with great service skills; it's a learned process. And what your people don't pick up on their own through work experience, life experience, or on-the-job training, or in other less formal ways, you'll have to give to them.

Many service companies have found that it helps to put all of their front-line service providers through a one-day workshop that explains the language and terminology of service management. This helps them understand their role in the organization and gets them to think in new and creative ways about how to best serve their customers.

Done correctly, these training sessions can really go a long way to help get everyone "on the same page" in terms of the company's commitment to the customer and how and why it's important.

Keep in mind we're not talking about the agonies of smile-training classes here. If you've hired the right front-line service people and the right managers and supervisors to guide them, there should be no need to force anyone to sit through any kind of training session that teaches them how to be nice.

Rather, these training sessions can open up a whole new world for some of your people. It's not unusual to hear them say, "So *that's* what the customer experiences when he or she comes through our doors" or "Here's a list of ten moments of truth I can think of that relate directly to the customers I serve."

Depending on how the training sessions are designed (formal one-day sessions, more informal half-day sessions, etc.), you can cover a lot of material in a short period of time. Just taking your people through discussions of your organization's service strategy, the moments of truth surrounding each customer contact, the Cycle of Service that uses those moments of truth, and how they can improve the way they serve the customer by becoming more involved in improving the systems is a good day's work.

Other training issues you'll want to cover include:

- Helping them describe, either verbally or on paper, what they see as their job duties. How do these relate to the customer? How do they fit into what the company wants to do? And how do they fit into what their coworkers are doing?

- Helping them write a mission statement for their work team, division, unit, or group, e.g., "As the kitchen staff, it is our mission to provide the best food."

- Discussing the power of teamwork and the concept of the external and internal customer as it relates to serving both groups.

- Analyzing the customer's mental report card; What's on it? What's important to him or her? How can we work hard together to score high marks?

- How to get feedback from the customer, what to do with the information, and how to respond to it.

- How to make suggestions about better service systems.

- How to deal with difficult customers—when to get help, and when to go to supervisors or managers.

- When and how it becomes okay to break the rules and become a customer's agent. How to be flexible, creative, and service-minded to meet the customers' needs, exceed their expectations, and still stay within the proper bounds of the company.

- How to feel better physically about the work they do—stress control, tips for feeling better at the end of the day instead of just at the beginning of it, etc.

- A careful explanation of what they can expect from senior management in terms of help, support, guidance, feedback, and, in effect, service from the executives.

This training is not just reserved for the front-line employees; their managers will need it too. It makes good sense to have your managers and supervisors attend the training along with their people—if not side by side with them, then at least as interested observers from the back of the room. Continuity is always important, in terms of the service vocabulary, the lessons learned, and the objectives of the training.

You'll also want to give your managers and supervisors their own brand of training that focuses on similar issues, but from more of a supervisory perspective. And the managerial training also should focus on systems changes, better operational procedures, staffing plans, and customer feedback initiatives.

3. OFFER SERVICE LEADERSHIP

A wise man once said, "Leadership is all about letting people work." In other words, it's not how smart *you* are, it's how smart you can make your people. Too many executives with a serious hands-on leadership style fail to keep this in mind.

If you've been schooled in the people-management method that says, "If you want something done right, do it yourself," then it's time to see why service leadership is just as much about empowering *you* as it is about empowering your employees and letting them do things when you feel they're capable of accomplishing them.

By one definition, service leadership can mean "leading those who serve by serving those who serve." In other words, you can make the best use of your time, energies, and talents by helping the people who deal with the customer—your managers, supervisors, and front-line employees—do their jobs to the best of their abilities.

You don't have to feel excluded if you're not involved in every decision made. Part of service leadership is providing your people with the tools and resources they need to thrive and then turning them loose to make their way.

By another definition, service leadership is also about modeling the type of behavior you expect to see in all your employees. This means that you pitch in and help with customers when necessary and show that you really enjoy the effort. It's hard for anyone in a so-called service organization to get behind the concepts of service excellence if they see their leader going through the motions, acting as if he or she is too important to work with an actual real-live customer or too busy to lend a hand when it's needed.

It's not too hokey to say that when the chief executive models the right service behavior with the front-line people, it gives them confidence and can even rouse their enthusiasm to higher levels.

There are scores of legendary stories of well-known and popular CEOs who loosened their collars, got behind the cash register, picked up the telephone order line, or walked the sales floor. These episodes, as brief as they may have been, serve a great purpose as employee morale builders.

Imagine how the front-line people feel when they can honestly say to themselves or each other, "Our leader really believes in giving quality service to the customer. He or she works just as hard as we do and helps us at the front line when we need it. I'll bet our customers would be surprised to know that the owner of the company helped them, but around here, it's a common thing."

While you don't have to spend all your time on the line with your service providers, they all want to feel that you know what it's like to be in their shoes. You don't have to be perfect at *their* jobs, just as they wouldn't expect to be perfect at *yours*. In the spirit of service and good fun, you can make your time with the customers and your front-line people enjoyable. Many CEOs find, to their delight, that it feels good to get back to their old ways, serving customers and meeting needs.

Because CEOs spend so much time making the big decisions, flying off to meetings at a moment's notice, or insulating themselves behind the doors of their executive suites, it's hard for the folks who do the customer service work to feel like there is much of a connection between the bosses and themselves. By working together with their people and handling the same challenging assignments the customers bring to them, many leaders can even rejuvenate themselves.

And all this talk about modeling the right service behavior is not just reserved for the front-line service people. It should rub off on the management staff as well. When Jan Carlzon announced his intention to turn SAS around through his commitment to a new service management program, he asked his managers to share his enthusiasm and act as his service-quality messengers. He knew he couldn't do it all alone, and he knew his managers could carry his message to their people in record time. They believed in him and brought his ideas and programs to the front-line people with a firm belief that he was backing them all the way.

And finally, service leadership is also about your ability to show your unflagging resolve in the face of tough times. The old joke about the kid who wants a horse for Christmas and digs through a huge pile of manure that ends up in his room says it best: "There must be a pony in here somewhere!"

Service leadership means that you can keep on searching for the pony even when you don't feel like it. Service to the customer is not static, it's dynamic. Everything changes, from what your customers want to what you can provide for them. Your people change, and the way you train, lead, and manage them changes too. And on top of this, your ideas, strategies, and systems change as well, sometimes for the better and sometimes for the worse.

True service leaders can keep on keeping on when things take a severe downturn. Business will not always be rosy and grand. You will go through down periods and, more likely, what seem like long "plateau" periods during which nothing bad or good seems to happen.

Now is the time to pump your own enthusiasm back into your service ideas, then work to rev up your managers and supervisors, and then work to motivate your service providers. Service leaders don't sit in their offices and wonder what will happen. They go out among their people and *make* things happen.

4. Create and Maintain a Collective Spirit of Service

This really means taking pride in your work as a service provider. Service spirit at your small business should be an attitude that says, "We serve our customers to the best of our ability, not just because it serves our interests as a company, *but because it's the right thing to do.*"

In recent years, some service jobs have taken on a bad reputation. For some people, who don't enjoy hard work anyway, a customer service job is demeaning, beneath them, or not worthy of much effort. If you get any sense of this in your organization, you should work to belay that attitude.

Service spirit is not about kissing up, bowing and scraping, or being servile; it's about helping people get what they want and feeling good about doing it.

Service spirit in your *employees* involves people who will:

- Try to be good to your customers, regardless of the situation.

- Take care of your customers' needs before starting on something else.

- Stop work on other projects to take care of your customers' needs.

- Go the extra mile and attempt to exceed your customers' expectations each time they deal with your company.

- Be patient, understanding, and compassionate with customers who may be having a bad day, not know what they want, or not know how to ask for what they need.

- Treat your customers like adults, not berate them, talk down to them, or otherwise make them feel that they don't matter to you.

- Not take customers' problems or complaints personally.

- Not try to pass the customer and his or her needs or problems off onto a coworker without at least trying to handle the situation.

- Add value to your customers' experiences with additional information, help, suggestions, or some other thoughtful gestures that make customers feel welcome and special.

- Get feedback from the customer, positive or negative, and know how to act on it.

Service spirit in your *company* involves the following elements:

- Executives, managers, and supervisors work hand in hand with their people to make sure service quality is a constant priority.

- The organization understands the customer's needs and the concept of the customer's report card.

- The organization solves customer problems with a minimum of bother for either the customer or the service employee.

- The management and the employees ask customers how they feel about the quality of the service they receive.

- The company puts the needs of the customer before the needs of the company—i.e., "It's not what important to us, it's what's important to the customer that matters."

- The organization gives its people at all levels the leeway they need to become their customers' agents.

- The organization will align its systems to be "customer-friendly" first and then "employee-friendly" as well.

- The organization will encourage feedback from everyone—customers, managers, and employees—about what works and what needs improvement.

- All levels of the organization will meet on a regular basis to discuss service quality improvements.

- The organization will do what it takes to win and keep the customer's business.

5. WEED OUT THE BAD APPLES AT ALL LEVELS

One bad employee on the front line can cause countless kinds of long-term damage, and not just to your company's reputation. Your assets, security, and future can be put at great risk if a ticked-off employee decides to turn his or her wrath on your company, customers, or employees.

We often see this kind of behavior manifest itself in what psychologists call "passive-aggressive" people. These are the ones who may be upset with you, their direct supervisor, a customer who they think insulted them, a coworker, or any number of other people, including their family or even themselves. But instead of attacking directly, they tend to work by subterfuge and discretion, hitting you or various parts of your company in devious ways. Some examples of these negative and destructive covert behaviors include

- Acting overly aggressive, unhappy, or angry on the telephone with a customer just to send a message that says, "The way I'm feeling right now is more important to me than what you want."

- Purposely losing customers by hanging up on them; using the telephone as a control or power tool; walking away and not returning from a face-to-face customer encounter; or purposely misplacing customers' orders, their money, the products they want, etc.

- Using service systems as a way to blame intentional mistakes on the customer or the organization, e.g., shipping the product one day past the customer's "must have it here" deadline; intentionally leaving out parts of the order; misdirecting other service employees with wrong directions, information, facts, figures, dates, or amounts; or failing to pass on critical information to either the customer or another employee who could have helped the customer or solved his or her problem.

If you want your hair to fall out or turn gray overnight, pick up a copy of *Sabotaging the American Workplace* (Pressure Drop Press, San Francisco, 1992). This scary book, edited by Martin Sprouse, consists of a series of interviews with mostly front-line service people who decided to—for lack of a better phrase—screw their employers. His book details one act of employee "terrorism" after another—sabotage; vandalism; stolen goods; missing money; employees who leave with keys; checkbooks, computers, software, data, and other irreplaceable valuables.

The reputation of your whole organization can be brought

down in flames by any combination of these kinds of behavior. And just a terrible attitude alone can cause customer confidence problems, bad publicity, negative word of mouth, no referrals, angry letters and telephone complaints, and, if it gets really bad, a stampede of customers over to your competitors.

The secret to keeping these so-called "terrorist" employees out of your business and away from your customers and employees is to heighten your awareness and realize that they exist—albeit, fortunately, in small numbers. Not every employee is bad, but the relatively tiny number of misfits can cause enough trouble to keep an army of your good people busy fixing problems, handling complaints, and attempting to salvage customer relationships.

While all of your employees are innocent until proven guilty, you need to raise your level of awareness about what goes on in your organization in terms of the way your people work with each other, their bosses, and the customer. Here are a few suggestions for keeping the good employees and filtering out he bad:

- Keep your finger on the pulse of the company, and ask your managers and supervisors to do the same.

- Hold your managers accountable for the work and behavior of their people, and demand that they make changes— job switches, discipline sessions, or terminations—when the signs point to trouble.

- Don't discount employee-about-employee feedback as a spurious awareness tool. What your people tell their supervisors and managers about coworkers with problem behaviors can be quite valuable. You must first create a team atmosphere that says, "We're all in this together, and what we do as individuals affects how we succeed as a team." Let the power of social conformity work for you as a behavior-changing agent.

- Offer rewards for good work, great attitudes, and superior service. Put the people who do lousy work, have a rotten attitude, and don't care about service on immediate notice: "We will not tolerate your anticustomer behavior here! Change or leave!" (As Green Bay Packers football coach Vince Lombardi so eloquently put it, "If you are not fired with enthusiasm, you will be fired with enthusiasm.")

- Know the difference between just bad service employees and terrorist service employees. You may be able to save the first group by changing their jobs; giving them additional support, feedback, training, or counseling; or even disciplining them. The second group is probably too far gone, and the sooner you relieve them of their duties in your organization, the better.

- Don't hesitate to fire noticeably toxic employees. Cut the deadwood, remove the people who live by a "can't-do" philosophy, and fire the ones who are trying to ruin what you and your hard-working employees have built.

- Once you've discovered their activities, don't allow terrorist employees to stay on board one extra minute. Their noxious behaviors can poison your good customers forever and make quasi-converts of your borderline service employees.

While this may sound ruthless, in some extreme cases it's completely necessary. You can save your company and your employees by being customer-committed and firm.

6. Model and Promote a Sense of Employee Empowerment at All Levels

The founder of Worthington Industries, John H. McConnell, sums up the stance his steel processing firm takes to support its employees:

> Pay workers well, treat them like people and expect them to work a bit harder than people who regard the boss as an antagonist. You have to trust the work force. If you don't you've done a bad job.[1]

McConnell's son, who is the CEO of Worthington, also takes a hands-on approach to the steel business. During his career, he worked in every phase of the business. The company's current president started on the steel-making shop floor, as did five of the company's nine vice presidents.

What's the point? Just that the other employees of this steel company know that hard work pays off—in promotions, in advancement, in new job duties, and, best of all, in pay and bonuses. The people who run this company are not afraid to get their hands dirty while doing some hard work.

As we've seen in the discussion of the concept of service leadership, the shop workers can look at many of the company's top executives and say, "He has been where I am and done what I do."

Another concept that relates well to empowerment is known as quality of work life. While this may be perceived as old hat to some of the more forward thinkers out there, it's just as important now as it was when it was studied so extensively in the 1950s.

Your front-line service people and your managers and supervisors want certain things from you. And many of these issues relate to how they feel—empowered, believed, trusted, cared for, and guided. If they haven't told you what they want in so many words, consider this a reasonable list:

- *We want to learn and grow.* Give us training we can use so that we can further our service careers for the good of ourselves and our company.

- *We expect justice and fair play.* No games, no secrets, no tricks, and no hidden agendas. Treat us like the citizens, workers, and family members that we are. Protect us from coworkers, managers, supervisors, or customers who seek to victimize us.

- *We want to get ahead on merit, not on favoritism or tricks.* Just keep the playing field level for us, so that we can compete and get ahead based on our accomplishments. Make the promotional and advancement systems clear, fair, and easy to understand. Reward us when we deserve it, and don't use the carrot-and-stick approach if we can never get our hands on the carrot.

- *We expect safe and comfortable working conditions.* Protect us as necessary from harm from hazardous things or people in the outside world, and keep us as safe as possible from harm while inside at work. Give us the resources we need to keep our machinery and equipment in safe working order. Provide some kind of security measures to protect us, our assets, and our property from loss, damage, theft, violence, or harm.

- *We expect fair pay and benefits.* We understand that you're running a business, not a bank. Pay us what we're worth, in keeping with the guidelines and standards of our industry. Give us a choice with our benefits, and make them as fair as you can afford.

- *We want to do meaningful work.* The way we grow and gain promotion and advancement is to show you and our management that we can perform well. Give us good jobs, and let us do them. Make our work as fulfilling as you can, and we will do the rest to make it good for ourselves. We realize that not every job will be enjoyable or perfect, but with good working conditions and clear, solid tasks before us, we will all prosper.

- *We want job security.* We realize that there is no such thing as cradle-to-grave employment. We also know that employee loyalty is a two-way street. If we feel that you're committed to us for the long run, we will commit to you for the same period. In lieu of layoffs in bad times, consider cutting our hours, switching our jobs, or changing our compensation rates.

- *We expect competent supervision and management.* Just as you don't want toxic, terrorist employees, we don't want toxic, terrorist managers or supervisors. It can be extremely stressful and difficult to work for a bad boss. Give us well-trained, humane, people-oriented leaders. Listen to our feedback if we all tell you that an employee should not be a supervisor or manager. You should be able to recognize the warning signs before we even have to tell you what's wrong.

- *We want to be informed and included in the decisions that affect what we do here.* Not everything you decide to do affects us directly, but we would like to have some say in the decisions that affect our service systems and the way we work with our customers. We will offer you feedback as to what we like and what needs fixing. We hope you will take our input into consideration before you make sweeping policy or procedure changes.

- *We want to be appreciated by our bosses, coworkers, and customers.* Not loved or worshipped (although that would be nice), but appreciated. We all like it when a boss, co-worker, or customer says, "Thanks. You did a great job." Serving the customer all day can be tough. Some encouragement and strokes along the way make it easier for us all.

Empowerment, like many other issues dealing with people, is a two-way street. You have to be willing to give a little to get a little, and so do your employees. By telling them what you expect and giving them a chance to live up to your expectations—and even exceed them, just as you try to do with your customers—you can create a strong and powerful sense of employee empowerment that works well for both sides.

7. MODEL AND PROMOTE YOUR SERVICE MESSAGE

Your mission is to develop a service strategy, making sure that it's simple and direct; fills in all the necessary details; is relatively easy to train, retrain, and review; and can go around your organization like wildfire.

This message should focus everyone's energy in the same direction and help begin the process—slow and steady, or fast and furious—of changing your small business into the *customer's* small business.

I've talked in great detail about what constitutes a good service strategy. I've offered real examples from actual companies, and I've invented a few of my own for discussion purposes. I've also shown you how to design a service strategy that fits your needs, but only up to a point.

How you design and write the service strategy that fits your organization best is ultimately up to you. Every small-business enterprise is different, even if you sell or deliver the same goods or services as your competitor across the street. You each have different backgrounds, business philosophies, managing and operating styles, and strong beliefs about what's important to you.

The trick to creating your firm's service strategy is to look around you and write what works for *you*. Don't copy the messages of other firms word for word and hope they will work for you. Be original and, above all, be thoughtful. Write words that will explain your message, that will inspire confidence in those who deal with you on all levels, and that will tell the world, "*This* is our company. *This* is what we feel is important to our customers and to ourselves. *This* is what we aim to do."

A service strategy of two paragraphs could take three weeks to plan, create, and draft. That's perfectly acceptable, as long as the final copy says what you want it to say and reflects the values, beliefs, and goals of your organization. Anything less is not enough.

While you should spend as much time and effort as you can to promote your service message to your executives, management and supervisory staff, and front-line employees, don't stop inside the walls of your company. The best company leaders are walking billboards for their firms. They tell the world what they're all about. They talk to their customers about service. They talk to the media and the business press about their service quality commitment, they advertise it, they give speeches about it to business groups, and they even let their competitors know what's going on.

If you think that sounds like an obsession with service, you're right. But before you say, "I could never do that" or "People wouldn't take me seriously" or "I don't have time for that," think about the most successful firms you know—large firms or small businesses, privately held or publicly owned, well-known or not— and ask yourself, "What has all this talk from the CEO about 'service' done for the company?"

The answer should be clear by now: It has brought customers into their places in droves. Nothing breeds success like effort. Look at it this way: If all their crowing about service quality and the power of the customer-focused business didn't work, would they still be talking about it? Learn for yourself from the service management pioneers around you. Talk about services, make it happen, and then step back and watch the results come pouring through your doors.

8. ASK FOR BETTER WAYS TO DO THINGS

There are always, always, always better ways to serve your customers. If you can't see them, look harder, and if you need additional input, ask first your front-line people and then your managers for their ideas.

As the discussion in Chapter 4 about the Cycle of Service showed, to get the best feel for how your company handles its customers at the many critical moments of truth, you should always start at the customer interface and work backwards. Begin with the moments of truth and the Cycle of Service for each of your customer encounters and say, "Now that we know what the customer experiences each time he or she comes here, what do we know about how to make it better?"

The answers will appear in your Cycles of Service, and if you've plotted these cycles carefully and thoroughly, they won't be hiding. Any fully formed cycle will tell you *exactly* what your customers go through each time you meet them.

And if you still want more information, go back to your best sources—your managers and your front-line people. Even the newest member of your staff at the customer level should know through trial and error, good instincts, and observation what works best for him or her and what serves the customer to the fullest.

When you can, promote the concept of *added-value service*. This says, "What can I personally add to the customer's experience to make his or her contact with me and our company more enjoyable, profitable, or even memorable?"

Once it takes hold, this idea of adding service value can have a highly synergistic effect on your entire firm. If each front-line service employee adds just *one* extra thing—a piece of helpful information, a money-saving coupon for the next visit, remembering the customer's name and previous order, etc.—to each customer encounter, think how many good things are happening to your customers all the time.

In the original 1947 Christmas movie favorite *Miracle on 34th Street*, you may recall that a large New York department store hired a man—who really was ol' Kris Kringle—to play Santa Claus. One day, as Santa worked with the children and their parents, the store manager was outraged to hear him tell a little boy and his parents, "We don't carry that toy, but you can go down the street to the other department store and find it there."

As the store manager was about to berate Santa for sending trade to the competition, he learned that his store's customers loved the idea that Santa could tell them where to find the gifts they wanted. This customer-friendly approach really says, "We're so confident that you'll like our store, our products, and our people that we know you'll come back again and again. We want to help you make good decisions, wherever you shop."

While I'm not encouraging your people to tell your customers, "Go and buy it somewhere else," there is a benefit to serving their needs with all the information at your disposal.

Think about the last time you went to a specialty store looking for a hard-to-find item. What happened when you asked the store salesperson, "Well, if you don't carry it, do you know where I can buy it?"

If that person was sharp and truly customer-focused, he or she said, "As much as I want your business, I want you to get what you need. Why don't you try the store around the corner? I know they carry what you're looking for. Please come back and see me if you need anything else and I'll be glad to help you."

The usual reality is, "Nope. We don't carry it, and I don't know who does." Besides sending the customer away with no extra help or information—since he or she must leave anyway to look for the item elsewhere—this close-to-the-chest attitude doesn't help the customer or you. There's a lot to be said for the value of information. Don't you think that the customer in the first example, who was told where to get the item, will remember where that helpful information came from? That's added-value service.

So don't encourage your people to be secretive. Everyone knows that there is always more than one place to buy what they need. If your people can provide information that serves the customer *now*, the chances are quite good that that customer will return to you for something else. And just imagine what kind of score you'll get on that customer's report card during the critical moment of truth with your service employee in your firm.

In service terms, most people do remember who helped them get what they want. It really is the little things that make a difference, and added-value service helps you put a name to a service idea that some of your competitors (who still use the "Here you go—Next!" approach) might forget.

Finally, your performance as a leader should also be subject to comment, scrutiny, and discussion among your managers and even your front-line people. Former New York City Mayor Ed Koch made the phrase "How'm I doing?" his calling card. He asked for feedback about his performance, and he got it. You shouldn't hesitate to ask the same question of all your employees.

And whether you gather the information personally from anonymous suggestion cards, or your managers collect feedback and submit it to you in a "no-names-please" report, or you hear things about what you do and how you're doing it from the customer, you should be ready to look at the information objectively and with as thick a skin as you can muster. After you've weeded out the pranksters, hostile messages, and other extraneous data, review the rest and see if you can make some changes for the better in your leadership style or operations.

It's hard to rate your own performance fairly, and sometimes it's even tougher to see past your own blind spots or built-in biases about how you work, lead your managers, and offer support to your front-line employees. But the legitimate information you receive can make you a better CEO, which is good for your company, your people, and of course your customers.

9. GET CONSTANT FEEDBACK FROM CUSTOMERS

As paradoxical as it sounds, you should relish all the customer feedback you can gather. Suggestions, complaints, and ideas that come straight from your customers are worth their weight in gold. Customer feedback is like the focusing knob on your corporate binoculars: It helps you see what's *really* going on out there.

In his outstanding book *Crowning the Customer*, Irish service management author Feargal Quinn, CEO of the Emerald Isle's Superquinn supermarket chain, puts it this way:

> The single most important skill you need to become truly customer-driven is the ability to listen.[2]

He should know. He and his supermarkets are legendary in Ireland for their customer responsiveness. He has created a very successful set of what he calls "Listening Systems" using customer panels, face-to-face feedback, and what he refers to as "welcoming complaints."

In fact, he looks at a customer complaint not as a nuisance to be handled with a heavy sigh, but as "part of an overall company improvement program that can turn them from being a cost burden to a *profit opportunity*." Quinn reasons correctly that whenever your customers complain, they are actually giving you an opportunity to *keep* their business. As a result, you also have an opportunity to make changes that can introduce new products and services you might have not thought about.

Each time someone complained about a slipping or failed system at one of his stores, Quinn took action. When one mother complained that whenever she sent one of her kids to pick up two or three items, the child was usually ignored. So Quinn created a small sign for children to carry that reads, "I'm shopping for my mum." With the sign in place, Quinn's service employees could see which kids needed help and would actively assist them in filling their mother's shopping list.

And feedback doesn't all have to be negative. Based on a customer suggestion, Quinn's produce managers labeled their fruit racks with ripeness signs that said, "Eat Now," "Eat Tomorrow," or "Let Ripen for Two Days."

Quinn is a fanatic about both service quality and product freshness. His bakers write the exact time of day each loaf of their bread is baked. Customers know when their heads of lettuce were picked and shipped to the store.

He created in-store "singles nights" for date-minded men and women. He built store-supervised playhouses and toy areas for the children of shopping parents. He established parking spaces for expectant mothers, developed special shopping carts for customers in wheelchairs, and even put pairs of scissors at each of his table grape stands when one woman told him she kept breaking her fingernails when she tried to separate the bunches. Now how's that for customer responsiveness?

Quinn puts his commitment to customer feedback this way:

In the long run, the most effective way to advertise the fact that you *welcome* complaints is by the way you handle them—word will soon get around. But in installing a new system for handling complaints, you do need to go out and sell it to your customers. Through notices, advertising, direct mail, or whatever medium is appropriate, make it clear that you welcome complaints as a way of improving your service. You also need to sell it to your staff, so that they see complaints as a service opportunity and not as a criticism of themselves to which they react defensively.[3]

There are literally scores of ways to collect customer feedback. Here are just a few, many of which you may recognize, use now, or otherwise have in place for the customer:

- *Surveys.* These can be written on the spot; mail-in survey cards; telephone in-bound, as in "Call this number to tell us what you think of our products or services"; or telephone out-bound, which involves telephone follow-ups after the customer has done business with you. Nissan is only one of many automakers who call all their customers after they visit the service department at a dealership.

- *Customer focus groups or panels.* These groups, gathered by professional research companies, or your marketing or other service departments, consist of five to fifteen current or new customers in a room with you. You should provide refreshments, snacks, and even a small gift as thanks for their participation. Tell your panelists that they can say whatever they want about your company, systems, products, services, or service employees. Don't react too strongly to the feedback you hear. Just make notes of what was said and meet later with selected managers and employee to discuss it. The theme of these focus group encounters should be, "Tell us how to be better so we can get better."

10. ALWAYS BE READY TO MAKE CHANGES, ADJUSTMENTS, AND IMPROVEMENTS THAT WILL CONTINUE TO BREATHE LIFE INTO YOUR SERVICE FIRM

In other words, don't rest on your laurels for longer than a minute. That sound you hear is your customers stampeding by as they head for greener pastures. You've got to catch them while you can, hold them, serve them in ways they never even thought possible, and make them want to come back for more of the same great treatment.

It's important to stick to the basics, like creating and following a strong service strategy, building reliable, friendly systems for your customers and your people who serve them, and putting your best service providers into position for that first moment of truth that appears on the customer's all-important report card.

And the basics should include a review of your ABCs. In the sales process, the letters "A-B-C" stand for "Always Be Closing." This idea says that you should start guiding your customer into a buying mode as soon as you can.

In service quality, "A-B-C" stands for "Always Be Changing." Your service strategy, service systems, and service people will demand your full attention. Give them what they need to fulfill your mission, and keep doing it forever.

Notes

1. Howard Rudnitsky, "You Have to Trust the Work Force," *Forbes*, July 19, 1993, 78-81.

2. Feargal Quinn, *Crowning the Customer*, (Dublin, Ireland: The O'Brien Press, 1990), 57.

3. Ibid, 106.

Chapter 10

Bending the Envelope: New Business Relationships You'll Need to Create to Survive

"Never learn to do anything; if you don't learn,
you'll always find someone else to do it for you."
—MARK TWAIN

Welcome to the age of partnerships and alliances. Whether you own a small small business, with only a few employees and one location, or a large small business, with several hundred employees and many locations, you are now entering a new era that might best be described as one requiring "compelled cooperation."

Whether you want to admit it or not, you can no longer operate independently. And in many cases, you'll find it to your advantage to develop relationships with other large and small businesses that you never thought necessary or even possible before today.

One of the new truths of small-business success is that you may not be able to service your customers completely without help. And today, this help can come from some surprising and previously untapped areas.

What follows are some new concepts you'll need to consider as you continue to plan your service management strategy, systems, and service-provider hiring requirements. At this point, as we near the end of the book, I'll talk rather bluntly in this chapter about the advantages and power you can create using leveraged relationships, new alliances with suppliers, and partnerships with your business allies to help make you both stronger. Your goal in using these cooperative efforts can be best defined this way: increased customer access through multiple marketing relationships.

▶ *That sounds complicated. Can you break it down further?*

"Increased customer access" is merely another way to refer to either getting more customers to come to you or getting your products and services to a wider range of customers. You'll want to develop relationships that introduce new customers to your business and vice versa.

The phrase "multiple marketing relationships" means that you don't have to "go it alone" any more. It's no longer necessary for you and your company to wear so many different hats—new product developer, marketing channel creator, advertiser, service or product deliverer, etc.

By expanding your horizons even a bit, you can discover unique relationships with people and companies on your periphery that can help you break new ground with your customers.

▶ *How about an example?*

For discussion's sake, let's take a quick look at a small-business partnership in which you aim to bring one product or service to new or existing customers and your partners aim to bring another. Together, you can generate, among other things, more buying power, better productivity, and better customer service through teamwork.

Let's say you own a small soap company and your new alliance partner owns a small towel company. You've decided to join forces and market your products together in the same package. He has a warehouse in your city, and it's full of towels. He buys his stock from a foreign manufacturer. You have a soap plant nearby that cranks out thousands of bars per hour. He wants to start a small towel-making operation inside his warehouse, offering a better quality towel and lowering his importing costs. You want to get your soap into more prestigious markets, to which he already has access with his towels.

With these value elements in mind, what options might you both offer to serve your mutual interests in the venture? (Get ready to think a bit creatively and outside the lines here.)

- Suppose your soap company is on a railroad line. Why not offer to store an inventory of his towels, so that you can package and ship the end product using your boxcars? In exchange for this, the towel company owner could introduce you to his best distributors.

- Why not offer to help pay for the towel-making machines? With your added investment, you can get a little better deal on the end product, such as a higher product markup for the use of your capital.

- Your new soap and towel co-venture will require more employees to run both operations. Why not agree to cross-train your respective employees in the ways of making and packaging both soap and towels? A group of these newly trained people could switch off and work at both plants over the course of the year.

- Each of you has have access to new and current customers—at both the wholesale and retail levels—that the other does not now have. Why not have your salespeople trade customer lists and go after these new groups?

- Why not create a luxury item catalog together, with product contributions from both sides? You can agree to handle the order-taking and toll-free number costs, if he pays for the printing and mailing costs for the catalog. You can split the cost of manufacturing and shipping the products.

Obviously, the possibilities are nearly endless; they are limited only by your imagination, your desire to take on new risks, and the strength of your working and personal relationships with the other firm and its leaders.

There are many lessons that we can learn from the soap and towel partnership, but one relates to our recent U.S. history of deal-making movers and shakers. One benefit of the merge-and-acquire 1980s was that it forced us to look at business relationships in new ways. Thanks to the buy-you and sell-me stance that forced dissimilar companies together, we've seen the value of new partnerships when these deals have worked out well.

We've even seen long-time competitors join together to sell their products and services. The isolationist, "You sell your stuff and we'll sell ours" stance has largely given way to a spirit of strength through alliance building.

SUPPLIERS: DON'T BITE THE HAND THAT FEEDS YOU

One of the first places to look for partnership relationships is with your suppliers. Those companies, large and small, that provide you with the goods and services you need to supply your customers with the goods and services they need can become your best friends.

➤ *The company, for example, that sells me my raw materials so I can make the final product is a potential business partner?*

Yes, and in more ways than might be readily apparent. But before we can look at how positive and cooperative supplier relationships can help your small business, we need to examine why this step requires such a large leap of faith.

History has not been kind to the usual buyer-supplier relationship. It's time for you to think more about the power in your supplier relationships and why a change in your treatment of your suppliers (and, you hope, their treatment of you) can benefit both sides. This, of course, means that the customer is the ultimate winner in the new partnership.

The usual management mindset most businesspeople have

when dealing with product and service suppliers is to try to get the lowest price out of them. And some businesspeople, especially those who work or own small businesses where the profit margins are thin to begin with, take this even more to the wrong extreme.

You've probably witnessed or experienced this mindset yourself. The buyer on the other side only wants to see your best price figures. He or she is not willing to talk about any of the other apparent or hidden value elements that may justify a certain price. When price is the only point of discussion, many sales relationships can deteriorate into "take it or leave it" deals where both parties go away mad.

The new trick to supplier partnerships is not to beat up on your suppliers by trying to drag every nickel out of them on your deals. You just can't go on playing the old buyer-seller, price-only, negotiating "bulldog" role that says, "I'm the buyer and you're the seller. All I want to talk about is price. That's the only option that's worth discussing right now. How low can you go?"

While this stance is certainly admirable from a blood-and-guts, cost-cutting standpoint, it's far too rigid to allow other options to come to the surface.

➤ *So if it's not just price and the cost of the deal, what else should I look for?*

Start by thinking harder. What else can your suppliers provide you besides a better deal on their products and services? Can they help you with service, delivery, or after-sale installation for your customers? Can they provide additional educational materials for you to give to your customers so that they can use your products and services better? Can they give you better deals on delivery, storage, or installation at your store?

Instead of demanding rock-bottom prices, is there anything *you* can provide your suppliers that will help them better serve you or their other customers? Can you offer help and advice on problems they're trying to solve? Do you have expertise that they need? Might you be able to trade your goods and services for theirs?

Stop looking at price tags and start looking at tradeoffs, barter deals, or swaps of data, information, storage space, hard goods, or services that you can use to make your suppliers more like your business partners. (And always keep in mind that many of your potential supplier partners are small businesses themselves. They may have the same fears, hopes, and goals as your firm. You may have more in common with them than with larger companies that do the same thing. There can be untold strength and camaraderie in this common ground.)

Obviously, if there are many suppliers in your industry to choose from, maybe you can indeed afford to be more aloof in your dealings with one of them. But if they offer a precious commodity or a valuable service that you must have, you may not be able to treat them in a cavalier fashion. This is especially true if you serve as a sort of middleman for your customers, taking your suppliers' goods and services, adding your own value, and then passing the finished product or service along to your customers.

Remember, there is more to any deal than just price. Look at it from your side as well. What if one of your best customers came to you and wanted to work out a deal that didn't just involve an exchange of his or her money for your goods and services? Would you go for it?

The concept of supplier-generated alliances is new and growing. Look at your own vendor accounts and consider whether it's time to change or upgrade the nature of the relationship into something that could be more profitable for both of you.

Suppliers as Information Sources

Believe it or not, besides just providing goods or service that you need, your suppliers can help you in a variety of ways. And you can help them as well. One way is through the exchange of information and key knowledge that makes you both better off.

Like you, your suppliers are looking for every edge, whether it comes from verified information, gossip, or even wild rumors. And, also like you, they've got their finger on the pulse of their customers (who are often your competitors), and they want to make them all happy. Since they have access to areas you may not, they can educate you about your customers, your competitors, and your marketplace.

They can give you an ongoing education about what is important to your customers, because in some cases, their customers are your customers too.

➤ *Why would they be willing to do that? Isn't it more likely that they'll keep quiet about things they hear?*

Business is all about information—who has it, who needs it, and who will go out and get it. Don't be shy about developing professional relationships with your suppliers that go beyond, "Stack it over there" or "We'll take three at the usual price."

Most people like to talk, and one of their favorite subjects is their job, their work, and the state of their profession. Encourage these discussions and reciprocate in kind. You'll be amazed at what you'll discover.

As an example, if you own a small grocery store, the potato chip, soda, and candy delivery people service your competitors down the street too. They hear things, see things, and do things inside your competitors' stores that could be extremely important to you.

Keep these additional issues in mind as you reevaluate the way you deal with your suppliers on an ongoing basis:

1. Some suppliers are in near-constant contact with your competitors; some are not. Those that are in a position to tell you important details about your competitors' prices, sales, personnel, or service or products changes, or to give you other valuable information that may reshape the way you do business.

2. Some suppliers are ready and willing to create co-venture relationships with you (or with your competitors if you're not ready or able to take on new risk) to develop "bundled" products or services that capitalize on the strengths of each

party. If they haven't asked you how you both might work together, ask them. Take the initiative to sit down over a sandwich with the executives at your suppliers' firms and brainstorm with them. You may be surprised to find that they have had similar thoughts and were just waiting for an opportune time to discuss it with you.

3. Some suppliers will educate you about new products or services they carry or ones your competitors now carry or are developing, keep you apprised of changes in your market or your industry, and let you know what customer feedback they are hearing, especially if you share mutual customers. As you should know by now, this last is critical to your success. You should always be on the lookout for customer feedback, regardless of where it comes from. And your suppliers can help you gather feedback data from your competitors' customers as well. You may be able to find out what is (or is not) selling well for them and adjust your sales and marketing strategies accordingly.

You know from experience that you can develop important business and personal friendships with the suppliers you see on a regular basis. No matter what the Internal Revenue Service says, plenty of bona fide business gets conducted over backyard barbecues, at ball games, and over business breakfasts, lunches, and dinners.

Solid, truthful, and, most of all, ethical behavior is critical in all of these types of relationships with your suppliers. Be honest and fair, and don't play one against the other. No amount of ill-gotten information is worth the loss of your personal reputation and that of your company.

You don't have to become best friends with these people, just good friends. Just like your customers, your suppliers want to know that you and your firm care for their needs. They realize that you have a business to run, as do they. And they understand that you won't always be in a position to buy everything they're selling every time.

Be ready to share what you know in exchange for what they know. Your information can be just as valuable to them, and you may have other sources they do not have. Fair treatment, a desire to help and not hurt, and a positive exchange of information can go a long way toward making you both stronger.

BUSINESS PARTNERS: DIRECT AND INDIRECT RELATIONSHIPS

Just as you can develop new relationships with your suppliers, you already may have other alliances with people and companies that are quite important to your customers. It's time to look at the impact—implicit or explicit—that these partnerships can have up your customers.

➤ *So these partnerships are not with my suppliers, but with firm that support my organization?*

Look at the following examples and ask yourself, In what ways do the external (paying) customers benefit from these relationships, and in what ways are they actually examples of failed moments of truth?

Airlines and Lost Luggage Delivery Services

Most large airlines contract with outside freight and delivery firms to deliver their passengers' lost and later recovered luggage items.

Typically it works like this: Finishing a vacation trip, you get on a plane in Los Angeles, bound for your home in New York City, with a stop in Dallas. Somewhere on the ground in Dallas, two pieces of your luggage get taken off your plane and shoved onto a flight bound for Cleveland. Arriving in New York, you discover, to your horror, that your bags are not among the ones on your plane.

The person at the airline's baggage claim desk has heard this sad story many times before and has empathy for your plight. She is polite and appropriately apologetic and, after making a few phone calls, discovers that your bags are at the airport in Cleveland.

She promises to have them put on the next New York-bound flight and delivered to your house the next day. She gives you the name of the freight company her airline uses to deliver passengers' bags, and you head for home.

The next morning, you receive a call from the driver from the freight company. He has your bags. Freeze frame for a bit: Here is where the following moment of truth can go right or not right. Here is where the airline's *choice* (and it is one, since there are hundreds of other freight and delivery firms that might want this contract) becomes critical, not just to you as the expected recipient of your bags, but to it as the *creator* of this business-partner relationship.

Back to our story. When the driver calls you, he will either make the whole lost luggage experience a positive moment of truth by saying, "I'm in your neighborhood now. May I come by and drop off your bags within the hour?" or "I'll be in your neighborhood somewhere between noon and four p.m. Will that be convenient for you?" or he will turn an already bad situation into a negative moment of truth by saying, "I'll be by with your suitcases somewhere between six a.m. and six p.m." or "If you're not there when I get there, I'll just leave them on your doorstep."

Or, in the worst case, he may just drive by your home when it's most convenient for him and (as I have seen them do) fling your bags onto your front porch, then drive off in a cloud of dust.

If the delivery driver takes the time to call and inquire about your availability, you'll probably feel better about the experience. After all, even though the airline lost your luggage, the delivery service is making a real attempt at being helpful.

Remember, as I have said on other occasions throughout these pages, it's not what's important or convenient to you, the service provider, it's what important or convenient to the customer, the service receiver.

And if the driver does not take the time to call you or unceremoniously tosses your valuable and even fragile belongings onto your doorstep, who, ultimately, will you blame? The delivery driver? No! If you're like most people, me included, you'll place the blame for this whole unfortunate and poorly handled moment of truth squarely on the shoulders of the *airline*.

"Why blame us?" howl the airline people. "We got your luggage safely back to your city. It's the fault of the delivery people."

➤ *So who is to blame for this service systems problem?*

The airline is primarily at fault first and foremost, because it chose to give the responsibility for an important service recovery function to this delivery service, not realizing that the delivery service was not up to the task of meeting the airline's customers' needs.

In this all-too-familiar tale, the airline has forgotten a critical service rule: Customers see what you show them. In the case of the luggage, they don't care that the truck driver was rude as much as they care that the airline company chose that firm in the first place. You need to be aware that the many business relationships going on in and around your organization often involve people who don't work *for* you, but actually work *with* you in meeting your customers' needs.

How well they do—often outside your firsthand observation or away from your direct notice—can have a tremendous impact on the way your customers grade you on their mental report cards.

➤ *Does this mean I need to consider my business alliance relationships very carefully?*

Absolutely. Consider the following similar examples where the customer's needs and expectations get handed from one service or product provider to another, with varying results.

The Music Store (that Sold You a Piano) and the Piano Moving Company

These are often two different companies with two very different goals. The first organization wants you to buy a piano. Although the salesperson may say all the right things, like, "Don't hesitate to call me if you have any questions or problems," or "We guarantee service after the sale," he or she is most concerned with the fact that your purchase of the piano means a nice commission.

The piano delivery company, if it works independently and isn't a part of the piano sales organization, has a completely different goal: To drive to the music store, get your piano into the truck, get the truck and the piano to your house, deliver the piano to the appropriate room in your house, and repeat the process one or one dozen times later that day at other piano-purchasing homes.

If the moving firm is truly customer-focused, it will say the same things about service after the sale as the salesperson at the music store, and will actually abide by them. The moving firm should be ready to tell the customer, "This is an expensive, high-quality musical instrument that should give you and your family much pleasure. Since we know it's valuable to you, we will take the utmost care and caution to get it safely into your home. We will move it carefully, taking great pains to avoid smashing your walls with it, dropping it, or otherwise damaging it in any way."

And if the music store and the piano movers truly see themselves as business partners, they both will exhibit this kind of care and concern for the customer and the product.

So who is in the driver's seat in this business relationship? Clearly, it's the *music store*, which, like the airline, can make a choice as to who delivers its goods to the customer. It is up to the store to choose wisely, and if that means it has to screen several delivery company candidates, so be it. Entering into a business relationship that affects the customer's report card to such a great degree requires something more than the typically haphazard approach that some firms seem to take when making business alliance and partnership decisions.

Let's look at another example where constant communication is the key to a high score on the customer's moments of truth report card.

Loan Brokers and the Banks where They Bring Your Loan Business

Thanks to rock-bottom interest rates, homeowners in the first half of the 1990s learned that they could refinance their existing mortgages and save hundreds of dollars per month in interest and principal payments. With loan rates on adjustable- and fixed-rate mortgages at their lowest levels in twenty years, the rush to refinance helped fill the offices of many banks, savings and loans, and mortgage brokers all across the country with eager customers.

When using the services of a loan broker, who is supposedly in business to find low rates, the homeowning customer comes in, discusses his or her current loan situation, and asks the loan broker to find a decent adjustable or fixed rate. And for his or her part, the loan broker hands the homeowner a stack of papers six inches thick and initiates a paper trail that, with luck, will end a few months later with a new and cheaper loan.

If everything goes smoothly and the loan-seeking customer's financial position is not the least bit out of the ordinary, it's possible to complete this task relatively painlessly.

The trouble appears when a "special" customer tries to go through this process. The special loan seeker may be self-employed, own rental properties, be going through a complicated divorce, not have all of his or her tax records for the last five years, or have some large or small glitch on a credit report that forces the loan broker to ask for even more paperwork.

And here's where the business relationship between the customer, his or her loan broker, and the bank, savings and loan, or finance company the broker chooses gets sticky. Any deviation from the norm—defined as two spouses with full-time, high-paying jobs, all their tax records and canceled checks since birth, and sterling credit reports—forces the loan broker to deal with an unrelenting, unforgiving, and inflexible lending agency.

Instead of trying to find an *accommodating* lender that will look at each loan application on a case-by-case basis, too often the loan broker just throws up his or her hands and tells the customer, "Sorry. There's nothing I can do. You'll have to submit more paperwork. Rules are rules, and the loan company needs some more stuff before it can make a decision."

And as the paper shuffle drags on for many months, the customer gets more and more discouraged and increasingly frustrated with what looks like a never-ending bureaucracy. The loan broker—who has dozens of other customers at various stages in the loan approval process—may just cluck his or her tongue and say, "If you want the loan, you'll have to give them what they need. It's out of my hands."

And in fact it probably *is* out of the loan broker's hands. But many loan brokers work repeatedly with the same banks and the same banking officers, and are hesitant to shop all over town for a better deal or a more flexible banker. They have become too comfortable in their business relationships, out of convenience or for other lesser-known reasons. However, this comfort and convenience certainly don't filter down to the customer. The loan broker knows that most people will just grit their teeth, climb into their attics or wade through boxes in their basements, and eventually come up with the required documents from the Eisenhower era.

This apparent apathy points up the fact that because the loan broker has not chosen lenders who are flexible or open-minded, the customer pays for the loan broker's poor choice. And since there are always new customers coming in the doors looking for loans, or other less-beleaguered customers who are near the completion of the loan process, the loan broker figures he or she can afford some negative customer feedback.

If you'll recall our discussion of service recovery, you know that "It's somebody else's fault" is not what your customers want to hear from you or your business partners.

Let's take one final look at the need for positive, customer-powered business partnerships. This next example illustrates the "greater good" idea that says, "When one of us succeeds, we all succeed."

Retail Shops in Partnerships with the Mall Owner

Here, the concept of all for one and one for all should reign supreme. Commercial or income-based real estate gives us one of the best examples of the need for strong business partnerships.

The mall operator certainly wants the shops in the mall to succeed. Too many vacancies are bad for business. Shops that come and go in less than one year's time are bad for leasing operations.

And for their part, each of the retail shop owners wants to succeed inside the mall as well. To do that, they may ask the mall owner to give them various lease concessions; reduced utility, security, or service rates; help with advertising or parking; or construction discounts.

For both sides to get what they want—a full mall and lots of business at the mall shops—each side has to see the other as a business partner. Although the mall owner doesn't sell your tennis shoes, he or she can help *you* sell shoes by making it easier for you to stay in business. This, in turn, should make you want to stay at your location and encourage you to sell, sell, sell.

Co-Venturing: Building Alliances Now and Forever

Now that you've seen the new significance of strong relationships with your suppliers and business partners, let's look at more of the benefits of these kinds of alliances. Working in tandem with carefully selected outside businesses like those described above can help you

- Get access to untapped markets.
- Learn new technology from others.
- Become more global-minded with your products or services.
- Develop joint technologies with partners who can bring additional capital, subject expertise, and even enthusiasm to the table.
- Get other companies to market your products to their customers, for which you pay them a royalty.
- Get other companies to market their products to your customers and pay you a royalty.

Alliance building is not always related to buying and selling. Sometimes there's strength in numbers. Two little firms can team up and kick the hell out of one big firm, figuratively speaking.

DOWNSIZING: IT'S NOT SMART TO CUT FOR THE SAKE OF CUTTING

For all this talk about partnerships and new working alliances, it also may be necessary to change some of the labor relationships back home at the company as well.

Cutting the number of employees in your firm is never easy. The number of euphemisms available these days to describe this less-than-pleasant task doesn't help to ease the sting much. Whether it's called "downsizing," "labor reduction," or just plain old "layoffs," having to say either, "You're fired!" or, more likely today, "There's no work for your position any more," the whole thing is tough, tough, tough.

But downsizing is a reality today, largely because cradle-to-grave employment, which was popular from the 1950s through the 1970s, is no longer possible. Further, even the biggest and most successful companies have had to face the hard, cold truth that while in the best of times, you can have many layers of management and some "soft" positions, where people stay on and do work that could be done by others, in the worst of times, these "placeholder" jobs are a waste of labor dollars and incur more costs than they're worth.

In the last ten to fifteen years, big businesses have learned what small businesses already know: You cannot function with too many layers of employees, whether it's at the management levels or on the front line with the customers.

Companies that had fifty vice presidents in the past now find themselves getting by quite well, thank you, with twelve. And so it goes on down the line from the senior executives to the front line; it's not only necessary to do more tasks with less personnel, it's now a survival requirement.

And for all the obvious negativity attached to the subject of letting people go, there's more to effective and humane downsizing than just swinging a collective axe. Not only does there have to be some sense of humanity attached to the less-than-pleasant process, there also has to be a good reason to do it. Making sweeping labor changes throughout any organization is like tinkering with the plumbing in your home; one change here makes for another change somewhere else.

The trick is to see the impact of the changes and how they go together. If you fire several people in the shipping department, will your customers still get their products on time? Will laying off dozens of people in your accounting department create problems with the way you pay your bills? These days, with so many service systems linked together, making major labor cuts in one area of the company can cause unanticipated problems in satellite areas.

But for all the apparent necessity of downsizing as a corporate survival tool, as expressed in the business press (especially in interviews with shellshocked CEOs and company presidents trying to justify their actions), cutting labor costs does not always automatically mean that you cut your total costs as well.

A downsizing campaign should be but one of many steps you take to save your small business from harm. Reducing the amount of dollars lost without changing the way the organization operates, won't change very much in the long run.

➤ *Labor is still an expense. Why won't a downsizing process lead to immediate cost savings?*

In too many cases, when a company's leaders (or machete-wielding personnel managers brought on board for the express purpose of doing something no one else wants to do) start firing everyone, removing so many bodies from jobs often hurts the growth of the company.

Downsizing should have a benefit for the company (since it does little for the people who are let go) that becomes apparent almost immediately. Are you removing wasted management levels, getting rid of service employees who are not the least bit customer-focused, or otherwise improving the overall efficiency and productivity of the company and providing specific cost savings, without sacrificing service to the customer? If not, rethink your downsizing policies to include the impact on the customer.

With regard to immediate cost savings, you may not see the results for several quarters. While that shouldn't stop you from doing what you have to do to save the company, don't expect overnight results.

In the meantime, consider the following advantages and disadvantages intimately attached to the subject of downsizing:

Pros

- It saves money—in some cases immediately, in others, downstream.

- It keeps marginal employees on their toes and puts slacking workers on notice that this could happen to them and that their job performance and attitude must improve.

- It can streamline operations at many levels.

- It makes the company more flexible in terms of responsiveness and objectivity, and creates changing rules, roles, and goals.

- It makes it easier to change policies and procedures; fewer people are affected.

- Smaller groups may work more efficiently and less bureaucratically.

- Smaller personnel numbers make it easier to redeploy assets and people.

- It may force or cause the owners or the senior executives to rethink the company's service strategy.

- In the long run, it may be better for the customers, since they may not have to wade through so many levels, policies, or procedures to get their needs met.

- It could help to improve the service systems and even the front-line service providers by cutting waste, streamlining operations, and even improving morale, especially if the remaining employees believe that the right people have stayed on and the deadwood workers have been eliminated.

Cons

For each of the real or hoped-for advantages of careful downsizing in the above list, keep in mind that the converse is also possible. Downsizing may not cause any real, positive, or cost-effective changes to take place. Here are some other downsizing disadvantages:

- It is often a painful event, for both the managers and the employees involved.

- Widespread terminations can suggest that the company may be headed for bankruptcy. True or not, this can have a devastating effect on the remaining workers' enthusiasm and productivity.

- It can ruin morale, even in hard-working, dedicated employees.

- It can cause innumerable conflicts inside the organization, as people fight to save their jobs.

- If it is not done with great tact and understanding, the company and its leaders can appear inhumane.

- Widespread personnel changes can have lasting ramifications for the long-term health of the company.

- It can affect the local economy where the company is located.

- It can cause employee factionalism, as departments band together in the hopes of survival.

- It can create specific systems problems that affect the way customers do or don't get their needs met.

- It can either create service gaps that don't get filled—at the expense of good service to the customer—or force the remaining people to do work they're not trained to do—which also can hurt the customer.

Any personnel changes you make, whether they involve hiring or firing, should be done only after a careful look at the ramifications for your organization's culture as well as the bottom line.

➤ *So where should this process take place? Aren't the front-line service providers most likely to be cut because of their numbers, lower wages, and relative ease of replacement?*

In tight economic times, some firms are quick to take a knife to the number of front-line service providers. This is often done in the vain hope that slashing lower-paying front-line jobs will somehow save big bucks down the road. And in their rush to cut service staff, some executives don't realize how much missing service providers can deprive the customer of a smooth trip through the company's many cycles of service.

Going to the other extreme and cutting large numbers of internal service providers is just as unwise as firing front-line service people. In any well-run service firm, the internal side of the company should work in harmony and in tandem with the front-line side. Each group has a mission—either serve the paying (external) customers or serve someone who does.

Removing key people from internal positions can throw well-oiled service systems seriously out of whack. There are critical internal roles that the customers may never see but that are still required if they are to get their needs met.

Besides the obvious morale and effectiveness issues, you'll need to consider the impact on the cycles of service and the many moments of truth that take place at the internal and external levels of the organization. In other words, if it ain't broke, don't fix it. If you can cut redundant staff positions or offer job sharing, early retirement plans, or other similar downsizing measures, look to those first. If not, downsize away, but do it in a thoughtful manner that takes into consideration more than just labor costs.

The San Diego Padres pro baseball team began a cost-cutting stampede near the end of the 1992 season. In an effort to trim their payroll from the $20-plus million mark to $12 million, team owners and top management traded nearly every star player in a matter of about eighteen months. This process, which was none-too-affectionately dubbed "The Fire Sale" by the critical media and howling fans, left the team a shadow of its former self.

And then the owners learned a business lesson that many service-oriented firms already know: If you reduce the quality of the product, your customers will go elsewhere.

And so they did in San Diego. After the moving vans took the team's best players away, attendance began to fall off. In the 1993 and 1994 seasons, people just stopped coming. Again, the management failed to heed the service rule that says that it's not what you want to see on the field, it's what the ticket buyer wants to see on the field.

Downsizing should never be easy or automatic. Look before you act. Why fire an entire department or several key service providers if their work is critical to the care and feeding of your best customers? While this sounds too obvious even to mention, some companies have not yet learned the old adage about winning the battle but losing the war.

THE POWER OF OUTSOURCING: GETTING MORE FOR YOUR MONEY

Now that the bad news is over, let's focus on another way you can bring qualified people into your organization without having to hire them as full-time employees. It's called *outsourcing,* and if done properly, it can save you not only time and money, but energy as well.

The idea behind outsourcing is to look outside your firm to fill specific needs that, in the past, may have been handled by specific employees or a whole department. Outsourcing helps you keep labor costs down because you can hire "outside" employees or companies on an as-needed basis.

➤ *So it's almost like having employees "on call" without paying them for full-time work, right?*

Any time you need certain specific functions that are now handled in-house, you may want to consider the savings, not just in dollars but in time, if you hire someone else to do the task.

For example, many small businesses have a difficult time handling all the paperwork, tax forms, deposits, timecards, and other minutiae surrounding employee payroll. If you have a midsize or large small business with more than five employees, chances are good that you must pay at least one full-time employee just to process the paychecks.

Some firms hire outside companies to process all the payroll information every two weeks, print the employees' checks, and mail them back to the office. These payroll processing companies often charge by the number of employees or take a percentage of the monthly payroll gross.

What makes this system worthwhile is that since their business is payroll, they know all the large and small details, the new and ever-changing laws, and the systems and steps they need to take to complete payroll chores carefully, accurately, and, most importantly, within the guidelines of the law.

And outsourcing the payroll function is just one of a number of ways you can use this cost-cutting technique. Some small grocery stores hire outside inventory specialists to count their merchandise each month. This saves them having to hire additional staff or pull people away from their regular work to complete this time-consuming task.

A small trucking business may not want to keep a full-time mechanic on staff. It can give a local garage a monthly retainer and work on a pay-as-you-go basis.

One of the best ways to implement an outsourcing program is to look at your own operation, pinpoint the most difficult, time-consuming, or expensive job, and then see if you can bring in outside people to help you with it.

Or, look at specific work functions you do only on an occasional basis and see if you can divert the employees who must do this work back to their original jobs by hiring outsource consultants to complete the work.

Consider the cost, paperwork, and efficiency benefits and use outsourcing to hire:

- *Temporary employees.* These may be needed during peak work hours, crunch projects, holiday sales, or other periods of increased work efforts.

- *Subject experts.* As in the payroll example, consider bringing in specific support firms to help you with areas where you may not have the time nor expertise.

- *Management consultants.* This is a classic outsourcing area, especially for firms that need expert advice on management, personnel, organizational change, operations, manufacturing, or any number of areas that require new and productive thought.

- *Seminar trainers.* There's no need to keep a full-time trainer on staff if you can look to the training and human resources development field for qualified outside trainers. These people can come in and create custom programs on any subject you want. They can teach your people, create train-the-trainer programs, and provide you with all the necessary training resources, educational materials, and support, all at fees based on the size of your company or the number of employees.

The key to effective outsourcing is not to look to the outside world for the solution to all your problems; there are some things you'll just have to tackle yourself. But with so many resources at your disposal, it is possible to bring in people and companies to take care of specific projects or problems, leaving you free to work on other important areas, such as how to serve your customers and keep them coming back for more.

But whatever you do, don't go overboard. Management guru Tom Peters puts it this way: "It's not a static world, for sure. Mindless outsourcing is dumb. Period."[1]

CAPITAL EQUIPMENT AND OTHER WHITE ELEPHANTS

In days of old, big was always better, and having lots of capital assets—machines, equipment, inventory, etc.—was often seen as a sign of robust corporate health. In this era of downsizing, making do with less, and changing roles in terms of partnerships, customer needs, and market share, a roomful of expensive assets is no longer a key to business success.

As a small-business owner in this position, you may need to rethink the way you deploy your capital assets. This is where the concepts of partnerships, alliances, and outsourcing really come into play.

➤ *You mean that instead of tying up cash and floor space with expensive equipment, we should look to outsiders to share the costs and use?*

The health-care industry offers a prime example of this need to develop external relationships with people who can help you serve your customers more effectively.

When was the last time you saw a ground-breaking ceremony for a new hospital in your city? If you live in a large metropolis, has not the trend been for a hospital to add on to its existing buildings or, in the worst case, sell its assets, name, or building to another larger hospital, or even close down entirely?

By nature, hospitals are highly capital-intensive businesses. The surgical rooms, intensive care units, specific treatment areas, and emergency rooms are filled to the brim with pieces of diagnostic machinery and equipment that can cost several million dollars each.

And yet, for all this modern technology, many hospitals are losing heaps of money because they have failed to meet the needs of their customers. Instead of going to the hospital for minor medical ailments or less-than-major surgical procedures, most customers (patients) go to their family doctor or a similar physician who specializes in their specific problem.

In-and-out medical procedures that used to require a one-night hospital stay (because that's where the equipment and the doctors were) are now done in outpatient clinics or other specialized sites away from the grounds of the hospital.

Therefore, many large urban hospitals find themselves with wings full of empty beds. And, just like a hotel with no guests, they're paying for those rooms whether they have customers in them or not.

What many large and bureaucratic hospitals' executive boards have failed to grasp is that their relationships with attending doctors are just like any other small-business relationship. Doctors who run their own offices, either alone or in partnerships with other doctors, are in fact small-business owners. The bulk of their work is done with patient-customers who come to see them, not at the hospital, but at their offices away from the hospital.

And since it is usually the doctor and not the patient who decides which hospital to use, the hospital that wants the doctor's business should work hard to cater to that business.

Think of your own health-care experiences or those of your family. If you or they needed a medical procedure that required a hospital stay, didn't you go to the hospital used by your doctor, rather than one across town? Rare is the patient who tells his or her doctor, "I want to go to hospital X. I hear the service is better." Since most of us as patients feel intimidated by the medical community anyway, we go where our doctors tell us.

But even at this late date, with the need for service thinking and service management all around us, some hospitals have still failed to grasp the concept that says, "Since we have all of this expensive equipment sitting here and depreciating like mad, why not go out of our way to encourage area doctors to use our facilities for their patient-customers?"

Instead, many entrepreneurially minded doctors have banded together to form their own general-practice or specialty clinics. Look in the phone book of your city and you'll see dozens of examples of physician-run small businesses: pain-treatment centers, back pain specialists, foot clinics, eye surgeons, prostate specialists, weight-loss doctors, fertility doctors, and any other specialty that no longer requires a hospital visit to receive the necessary consultation, tests, or treatments.

As small-business owners, these doctors have realized there is strength in numbers and that it's not necessary for them to spend their scarce dollars (especially in their early practice-building years) on expensive high-tech equipment if they can get access to it in other ways.

And the health-care field is not alone in being capital-heavy. Airlines also get saddled with older, outdated, or even mothballed equipment. They have had to come up with unique and cost-effective ways to replace their fleets. Unlike the federal government, which can park unused Air Force planes, Army and Marine tanks, or Navy ships somewhere and forget about them, the airlines must buy new flying stock at regular intervals, based on the flight hours each plane accumulates.

Storing an aging piece of aluminum, glass, and steel in a hangar may work if you only have a few planes, but in the larger firms, there may be dozens of old planes to unload. So what do they do?

Again, partnerships and alliances can offer solutions to capital equipment problems. Some airlines sell their older planes to small countries, which may retrofit them and put them back into service. Others turn their old planes into cargo ships and sell them to air cargo services, either for a flat fee or for a percentage of the smaller firms' business.

And even banks, which used to pride themselves on having a branch on every corner, have discovered that as their customers move more toward direct deposit, ATM banking, banking by mail, and even computer and telephone banking, they no longer need so many physical locations. What started out as a way to provide customer convenience—branches near our homes and workplaces—has become a real estate liability.

Many banks find themselves stuck with a number of buildings they can't operate profitably or sell for a profit if they were empty. Like their counterparts in health care, bankers have found that their customer bases have changed; they have migrated to new or different services, or otherwise changed their banking habits.

Smart banks have moved with these changing times, offering account services and conveniences before their competitors do. They've moved away from the monolith bank building concept or the "branches everywhere" philosophy and concentrated their marketing and new account efforts in more profitable operations that don't require such capital-intensive real estate holdings.

You can see from all this that the playing field has changed and will continue to change. It's now necessary to look outside your doors and see who can help you get where you want to go. Some firms have made the trip and will welcome you along. Others are in a position similar to that of your firm and will want to work with a company and leaders who share their goals.

Do begin to look at your exterior relationships with an eye on teamwork and the strength of a shared fate. Your customers are already looking at your business relationships anyway. Why not make them the best they can be?

Notes

1. Tom Peters, "Contradicting Myself 13 Ways," *Forbes ASAP Magazine*, Spring 1994, 136.

Chapter 11

Getting Back to You: The Service Leader

"Leadership is *action*, not position."
—DONALD McGANNON

This chapter is all about responsibility—who takes it and what it means. Service programs often fail because of credibility gaps. If top management is committed to the program but can't get the middle managers or front-line service people to come aboard, the program will usually flop. And if a dedicated core of middle management motivators can't get much of a rise out of the executive level, the program probably will die off after a few half-hearted months. Lastly, if the front-line service people don't get a solid sense of support or don't back the service idea either, not much good can come of anything.

The key to service success ultimately starts and ends with the business leader. Have you bought into the principles of service management? Can you take on the personal challenge to change the direction of your entire company and make it stick? Is your new frame of reference *service leadership*?

Is your service strategy your credo, purpose, and reason for being in business? Service leadership starts at the top. Can you buy into the service quality idea and inject the rest of your organization with your enthusiasm? Do you have the physical energy needed to serve as the service "billboard" for your people and your customers?

Are you capable of changing—personally, philosophically, "managerially," and professionally—in order to make your small business truly service-driven? Who will help you as you move in this direction of meeting the customers' needs?

Can you ask for help from your managers, service providers, and customers as you go? Are you willing to nurture your "true believers," remove the toxic "service saboteurs" from your management or front-line ranks, and staff your firm with the best people you can afford?

Finally, are you ready and willing to say, "Here's what we're going to do, and here's how we're going to do it" starting right now?

Positive changes must take place for you to grow and thrive. If you're not willing to make changes in the way you see your customer and serve him or her, don't gripe about lost opportunities, missed business, or a bad economy.

THREE INGREDIENTS FOR SMALL-BUSINESS SUCCESS

As one harried small-business executive puts it, "If I see one more business article or business TV news story that says, 'It's time to do more with less,' I'm going to scream. We've been doing more things with fewer resources for years."

Welcome to the real world. As a small-businessperson, you've probably got a few scars and bumps from trying to get by with less. Cutbacks are a fact of business life, not with just people, but with materials too. You may not want to hear it again, but here it comes: You *do* have to get by with less.

Fortunately, you can get by with less and still make great profits, have great people, and run a great small business. You only need healthy doses of three key success factors: brains, guts, and luck. While it's hard to measure these important quantities, they're equally important for your survival in the small-business marketplace. And the further good news is that even if you don't have equal amounts all of the time, enough of one of them will still carry you along.

Brains

This one's a given. You must be smart, and you must surround yourself with smart people. While you may be able to skimp on the style of furniture in your office, don't cut corners with people. You should handpick your executive staff for diversity in all areas, especially creativity and flexible thought. While IBM may prefer its people to wear dark suits and white shirts, conformity is not always linked to creativity. And old story illustrates this:

A chief executive was taking one of his friends on a tour of his facilities. As they passed one office, the guest looked inside to see a man leaning back in his chair, with his hands behind his head and his feet on his desk. He appeared to be daydreaming. Surprised to see this behavior taking in place in front of the owner of the company, the friend said, "How come you let him get away with that? He looks like he's just doing nothing."

As the CEO continued down the hall, he said, "That man in there is paid to think for me. He came up with one idea that saved us one million dollars. I let him do his job any way that works best for him, because, in the end, it works best for us too."

There's also an important distinction to make between having brains and being smart. It's like the highly-intelligent scientist who can solve problems related to astrophysics but can't remember where he parked his car. Don't confuse IQ points with real intelligence. There are many people who make up what they lack in book-learnin' with good old-fashioned common sense. And in small-business operations, a little common sense can go a long way with the customer.

And having an extra dose of common sense can keep you from making mistakes or decisions that sound good to just you and not your company or the customer. This also reflects the added benefit of keeping bright men and women by your side. Every good leader needs sounding boards. These are the people who can take your ideas, work them around in their own minds, and then give you their opinions about what they think will work and why.

As always, to paraphrase Harry Truman, the final decision

should rest with you. But it never hurts to hear your people give their unique perspective on what you have put on the table. They are influenced by their own experiences and histories, just as you are. And the closer they are to the customer, the more they will know what the customer wants.

Guts

Another necessary ingredient, guts is defined as the internal fortitude you need to make tough decisions and keep going in the face of tough times. Guts is obviously related to risk taking, and most small business leaders know this subject intimately.

Unless an elderly relative left you millions of dollars and the order to go forth and start your own small company, you probably began your operations on a budget more equivalent to a children's lemonade stand. Tales of booming businesses that began in garages, warehouses, home kitchens, and home office-bedrooms are common in small-business success circles. There is a real value to these stories because they help illustrate one thing: *It can be done, and these people did it.*

Guts and risk go together because taking on the latter requires much of the former. All business is risk, and the best small business leaders know the difference between smart risk and dumb risk (See the need for Brains from above.) As they probably will attest, learning this difference was not without its hard times, learned lessons, and occasional uses of the phrase "I'll never do *that* again!"

Guts is what says, "Let's change our entire operation and aim it right at the needs of our customers. Let's create a service strategy that tells the world what we do. Let's set up ways to make it so easy for our customers to do business with us so that they'll come back frequently. And let's tell our people it's okay to think like customers think and do what's necessary to meet their needs and beat their expectations."

Guts is also what says, "This is the path I have chosen for our organization, and we will live or die by it." And guts also tells everyone in the company, "We will not fail for lack of our effort."

Luck

This last important ingredient is just as necessary as the other two, if not more. You can be smart and gutsy, but if you don't have any luck, you probably will fail. You can be dumb and gutsy, and if you're missing luck, you will certainly fail. And if you have no brains and no guts, all the luck in the world won't save you. Just as we use pepper as a spice for our foods, not as a main ingredient, luck is a condiment for your small business. Luck also consists of fate, good timing, and being in the right position when opportunities come along. Here's to hoping that luck is sitting over your shoulder and waiting for the right time to arrive for you.

Brains is all about seeking opportunities, putting yourself in the right paths, meeting the right people, and asking others to follow your plans and ideas.

Guts is all about movement. You must be willing to get out and see what's around you and how you can improve or change what you've observed. It's also about taking chances when you think the odds are in your favor and even doing it a few times when they are not.

And luck is all about those happy instances where the cosmos lines up and you get something you've always wanted and never thought you had a chance to get. It's a rare commodity; the more you have of it, the more you want of it. Like brains and guts, you can't hoard it, buy it, or get it from your local store. It all comes from within, and if you've already arranged your small business in the right ways, it will come along, probably when you least expect it and need it most.

If anyone ever points to your thriving small business and asks, "How did all this happen?" you can honestly point to these three old friends as the ones who put you where you are today.

NEVER GIVE UP, NEVER GIVE IN

These are the economic times that try small business people's souls. According to some happy statistics from our friends at the Small Business Administration, 62 percent of all businesses dissolve within their first six years.

In their 1992 report, "The State of Small Business," the SBA found that, for the general category of "service businesses," 75 percent of them made it for at least two years; 46 percent made it for at least four years; and 37 percent made it to at least six years. These glowing numbers could point you in a dozen different directions as to why. The easy answer is this: You had better start strong and keep on getting stronger.

Until recently, this "survival efficiency" hasn't always been a number-one priority for many small-business leaders. Martyn Hodes, a San Diego-based advertising executive and owner of Mesa/Copy, puts it this way:

> The average small business owner or operator must concentrate first on the product or service, then on marketing it, and then on keeping sufficient capital to survive until the first two kick in. If they get hooked on fads or the "subtleties" of management at the expense of those three elements, that is, before the company has proven its basic viability, it's on the road to oblivion. And while the large corporation can take a wrong turn and then come back, as history has shown us, the little guy seldom has the reserve for a bounce back. Of course, once the small business has proven it can survive, top management should already be thinking about new and better ways to run the company.

But here's something else that's positive to keep in mind as you work another day. You can't compete with the big guys on the Fortune 500? So what! According to management futurist author John Naisbitt, the so-called Fortune 500 companies are actually not the economic force to be reckoned with that you might think. In a March 1994 interview on PBS television, Naisbitt said, "All told, the Fortune 500 companies only account for about *10* percent of our U.S. GNP." This hardly makes a dent in what small and midsized businesses contribute to our economic health as a nation. So go out and give yourself the credit you deserve.

Who cares if the business media don't interview you, profile your firm on their covers, or otherwise treat you as the third coming of Henry Ford? We all know who creates most of the jobs in this country, pays plenty of the business taxes, and stimulates the economy with growth, new products, and service to its customers.

THE MYTH OF THE OVERNIGHT SUCCESS

Many people who look at small-business success stories often fail to see one of the main yet hidden ingredients for success: time. What appears to have risen like a service phoenix in the last six months or year was probably a company whose leaders and people have been hard at work for ten or even twenty years. There are very few small-business flashes in the pan. Success demands hard work, and that takes time. Another way to put it might be, "All things come to those who wait (and make careful, solid initial plans and ongoing adjustments)."

Nothing happens overnight in business except the mail run. Things take time to develop properly, and in many respects, there's not a lot you can do to rush this process. Service quality, through changes in your company, will not happen overnight either. Depending on the longevity, health, strength, and direction of your small business, it may take months, or even years for you to put your finger on the exact time where a noticeable, positive turnaround took place.

It's the same with any small business service quality program—these things take time. There is a fine line between allowing a program to fester, rot, and die and allowing it to run a course of growth and development. One of the things that makes you better than the big guys is your ability to move with the times, and do it rapidly. You can make required adjustments, often on the spot, that might take the corporate giants two years and two thousand meetings to decide upon.

And since you're small, time is hardly a luxury for you either. You also have to be better and faster than the big guys. But mobility, flexibility, and fewer management layers make this easier, too. Instead of a conglomerate with 182 vice presidents, all of whom report to different departments and do different things, you might have only seven, or three, or one, or even none. When you signal a change, it can hit their desks within days, if not hours.

Time is also a factor in terms of training all your employees at all levels to understand their roles and duties in a service quality program. Even if you only have twenty-five people, it will still take some significant amount of time to train them all. You have to account for scheduling problems, the need to continue offering high-quality service to the customer while this training takes place, and time for this new training to sink in.

From experience, I know that the logistical side of employee training involves much behind-the-scenes, preclass work even before your employees arrive. It takes time to prepare the training materials, organize the classroom participants, set up the training facilities, and then give the actual training. Feedback and follow-up training, which should be a part of any training done by your in-house people or outside consultants, is also a time-consuming process.

All this is not to say that just because training takes time, you shouldn't pursue it. On the contrary, you *need* it in order for any service quality initiative to survive. New ways demand new training. And if your small business is truly progressive, employee service training will be just part of the frequent and ongoing job training you give your employees now.

This is not an area you should leave to chance. If you have good in-house trainers who can create and present the service material you need to make your people customer-focused, put it to them and ask for their plan. If you don't have an in-house training capacity, there are a number of qualified service management and front-line service training firms who can offer off-the-shelf, custom, or turnkey programs to meet the needs of your company and who know your specific industry.

Look at it this way: The time to train your employees to be customer-focused should be before the first customer even walks through the door, calls, or sends in an order. So since you probably don't want to go back and reopen your business, just consider today and every day that follows an opportunity for your people to build and enhance the customer skills they have now and to fill in the gaps with good training.

Business Life Cycles: Where Do You Fit In?

When you consider more about this "overnight success" idea, you should be able to find your own small business somewhere along the following service success time line. The descriptions are not perfect; you may find your firm in one of them or in transition between two. The value of understanding these various stages comes from knowing where you are and where you want to go.

Survivor-Group or Individual Stage

Here, the company is at the founding stage. One or more highly motivated entrepreneurs have formed a work group and have decided to make a go of their ideas, dreams, and plans. Since the company is small, the work is usually equally divided, with certain people tending toward their strengths and avoiding their weaknesses. The hours are long, the future is unclear and uncertain, but there is much hope to be had. At this point, the company is idea-strong and resource-weak. It needs two very important C's to survive: cash and customers.

Family or Growing Stage

At this second stage, the company founders and leaders have found some cash and some customers—at least enough to keep the doors open and move the business from a low-tech, low-maintenance, "backyard" operation to an office, factory, or retail setting. They've hired some managers, some support people to staff the internal customer positions, and some front-line service providers. There are now more assigned duties and departments then before.

The leadership style still has plenty of entrepreneurial spirit, and there is still a level of business informality that says, "All for one and one for all."

At this point the company is growing, expanding, and changing before the eyes of the leaders and founders. Some service systems need to be overhauled or created from scratch, and it's time to look at the original service strategy to see if it needs an adjustment.

Village or Expanding Stage

By now, the company is making money steadily. Service to existing customers is now a critical issue. There are more "official" layers of management, and certain departments exist to do certain things.

Work continues at a feverish pace, and there is even a sense that the company has taken on a life of its own. It's time to look hard at the service systems to make sure the leaders and managers are getting the best out of their service people as they help the customers.

Feedback from customers becomes important, and the information-gathering process for employees and customers should be in place to track the data. There may be steady talk of opening other divisions, stores, or branches away from this main one, and training, staffing, and logistics also become critical discussion points.

City or Mature Stage

In this fourth stage, the company has finally "arrived." It's proven to all that it's in it for the long haul, and with this success has come a myriad of systems, personnel, and strategy problems. The little kid has finally grown up to be an adult.

There are departments and department heads to handle the administrative, customer, and customer-support functions. The company's leaders and founders are now busy with planning and direction decisions and may not have much hands-on time. They tend to be caught up in activities that take them away from the customers.

At this point, it's vital for the founder and top executives to step back and make sure they are still meeting the original goals they had in mind when they started the business. It's also time to take a look at the way the customer passes through the organization and make sure the critical moments of truth and Cycles of Service accurately reflect what is going on at the front line.

Management training, employee training, and ongoing "reality" checks about the customers' health and happiness are now undeniably necessary.

Metropolis or Resolution Stage

Many of the same requirements for the previous stage also apply to this level. By now, the company is anchored in one spot, in terms of its long-term survivability. Barring a major catastrophe like a stock market collapse, a government indictment, or a financial blunder of epic proportions, the company will weather future storms and continue to grow and develop in a variety of different directions.

While it may appear to the founders or leaders that the company nearly runs itself, now is not the time for a hands-off style. Constant adjustments are still necessary, but thanks to the firm's health and relative longevity, these changes are not nearly as sweeping as during the initial stages.

Wherever you fit on this scale of small-business development, you can see that no matter what the stage, you still have to work hard. Advancing from one stage to the next may be part of your long-term goals, or it may happen just as a product of time and development. Since you can't really force the process, as you stay within each stage, look at the parallels between the stages; each one is still about attracting, serving, and keeping customers.

LONG-RANGE PLANNING: THE NEWEST MEMBER OF JURASSIC PARK

As we are slowly learning today, there really is no such thing as long-range planning, at least not the kind that is still taught in our M.B.A. diploma factories, otherwise known as Harvard, Wharton, Cornell, Stanford, University of Southern California, and the like.

And as your own experience will surely attest, long-range planning for many small businesses goes no farther than the next six months or, more likely, the end of the fiscal year you happen to be in. Rather than focusing their efforts on long-range plans for the next year or five years, wise small-business leaders challenge themselves and their associates to emphasize the best long-range *responses* to changes brought to them by the marketplace, their competitors, outside influences, and, of course, their customers.

Looking forward is perfectly acceptable and even necessary to help you change, adapt, and grow. Just don't look so far ahead that you fail to see the speed bumps, potholes, and black ice on the road in front of you. In some organizations that have created ad hoc or even semipermanent planning committees, groups, or teams, after these groups have been in operation for a few months, top management discovers that they have spent precious time and piles of assets trying to justify their existence. Instead of banding together when necessary and coming up with workable short-term solutions or ways to capitalize on pending opportunities, they set about creating 100-page reports, additional subcommittees, and lofty recommendations that will require more input from—you guessed it—the planning committee.

Don't abolish your plans; abolish every unnecessary planning group that doesn't give you timely answers backed up by research, customer and employee feedback, and their own sense of what will work now and later for the customer.

Some Final Thoughts

What have we learned by this stage in the service revolution? For some small businesses, the answer may be "not much." Looking at the ebb and flow of customers into and out of many organizations, much of the interaction and the "business of business" seem to happen by accident, luck, timing, or because one party needs the other. Each day, as you brush your teeth in the morning, before you grab your work-laden briefcase and head off to work, keep asking yourself this important question: *"Who are our customers and what do we really know about what they want?"*

The fact that you won't always know shouldn't alarm you. Be prepared to do your homework, ask questions of every customer you can reach, get advice and feedback from your employees, and never stop learning.

Customers' needs and expectations are changing all the time. Just the fact that they will leave you even if you give them *good* service demonstrates their desire for and expectation of *excellent* service. Always be changing your firm and your operations to match these expectations as best you can. And give some of your personal power back to your front-line service people that so they can act more on their customers' behalf.

Keep developing new strategies for your business as it changes, which it will certainly do. This subject can be the driving force for your business if you guide it correctly. There can't be any half-baked attempts at smile training, quick fixes, or change not backed by a top-down commitment from above.

And have your service management tool belt handy as you go back to the basic ideas, themes, and messages you want to get across, both to your employees and to your customers.

This book has tried to drive home one lesson: The customer-powered, service-driven, service-quality-obsessed small business starts and ends with meeting the needs and exceeding the expectations of your customers. Do what you can to make this a reality by creating the right service strategy and the right systems, and then letting great service providers carry your message right to your customers.

Notes

1. Karl Albrecht and Steven Albrecht, *The Creative Corporation*, (Homewood, Ill.: Dow Jones-Irwin, 1987), 20-22.

An Afterword for the Small-Business Owner

The following cry for help described below is not new. You may have seen it in Ann Landers' advice column, reprinted in your favorite business newsletter, or any number of other published places. Don't let this short little story fool you with its simplicity.

This modern epic just happens to boil down all of what Tom Peters, Karl Albrecht (and even Steve Albrecht), Jan Carlzon, Ron Zemke, and the remaining short and long list of other noted service experts and authors have to say about failing to give your customers what they want, meeting their needs, or exceeding their expectations. I can only guess that you will groan in agony if you discover similar things taking place at your company.

REMEMBER ME?

I'm the person who goes into a restaurant, sits down, and patiently waits while the waitress does everything but take my order. I'm the person who goes into a department store and stands quietly while the salesclerks finish their little chitchat. I'm the person who drives into a gas station and never blows the horn, but waits patiently while the attendant finishes reading his comic book.

Yes, you might say I'm a good person. But do you know who else I am? I'm the *Person Who Never Comes Back*, and it amuses me to see you spending thousands of dollars every year to get me back into your store, when I was there in the first place, and all you had to do to keep me was to give me a little service and show me a little courtesy.

—from a Better Business Bureau Bulletin

Now that you know how the unserved customer feels sometimes, it's time for a little encouragement. Read the following with your own small business in mind and see if it doesn't motivate you to work a little harder and a little smarter:

You cannot bring about prosperity by discouraging thrift. You cannot strengthen the weak by weakening the strong. You cannot help the wage earner by pulling down the wage payer. You cannot further the brotherhood of man by encouraging class hatred. You cannot keep out of trouble by spending more than you earn. You cannot build character and courage by taking away man's initiative and independence. You cannot help men permanently by doing what they could and should do themselves.

—ABRAHAM LINCOLN

If that's not a good example of the Small-Businessperson's Credo, I don't know what is. The true, hard-working spirit of every small-business owner or operator is captured in Abe's words. In so many ways, he says, "Lead by example. Model the behavior you want to see in your employees. As you strive to make positive changes in your service strategies, systems, and employees, don't expect the people around you to guess what you want them to do. Lead the way as you make things right. Your employees have expectations and needs just like your customers. And because they both expect you to help them along the way, you are more of a service provider than you know."

According to numbers from the Small Business Administration, in the 1980s, small business firms created more than 60 percent of America's net new jobs. And these numbers are getting bigger in the 1990s, and they're expected to increase as we near the end of the decade as well.

As columnist Fleming Meeks put it in the 1993 *Forbes*

"World's Best Small Companies" issue, "So it's left to the smaller companies on their way to becoming big companies to create the bulk of any society's new jobs."[1]

He continues to suggest that small businesses as a group have more power, flexibility, market acuity, and more dynamics with their people, products, and services than their larger counterparts. But he voices a caution that should not be lost on our politicians, bankers, stockbrokers, economists, analysts, and new and ongoing entrepreneurs: "An economy that fails to nurture smaller companies to replace the stricken giants is an economy condemned to stagnation."[2]

So consider yourself and your company to be a very valuable part of our economy. And never forget we're living and working in a service economy; you're a part of it just like any other large or small firm. You have something to offer our economy and, with hope, our society.

A good small business attracts good customers, good employees, and good success. Your journey will take you onward and upward, with a few falls and plateaus in between. But the fact that you're already committed to making your own living is a clear signal that you can accept the challenges ahead.

Notes

1. Fleming Meeks, "The World's Best Small Companies," *Forbes*, Nov. 8, 1993, 219.

2. Ibid.

Appendix

Small-Business Groups, Publications, and Resources

American Society for Training & Development
1640 King St., Alexandria, VA 22313
(703) 683-8100
This well-known HRD organization is devoted to the needs of all employers, particularly human resources, training, and personnel professionals; publishers of the well-known *ASTD Journal*.

Better Business Bureaus
The BBB is a long-running service organization whose members include many small-businesspeople and companies across the country. They serve a unique function as a sort of "seal of approval" for customers who may be looking for a place to take their money and time. Check your telephone directory for these groups in your local area.

Entrepreneur Magazine
2392 Morse Ave., Irvine, CA 92713
(714) 755-4121
This monthly magazine is dedicated to the needs and desires of the small business entrepreneur. The articles and advertisements are geared toward people who want to run their own businesses. The firm also publishes well-researched start-up guides for literally hundreds of small businesses.

National Federation of Independent Business
Washington, DC
(202) 554-9000

Founded in 1943, the NFIB is this country's largest advocacy group representing small and independent businesses. The organization features more than 600,000 members from high-tech, retail, service, farm, and manufacturing industries.

It was created to give small-businesspeople a lobbying voice in government decisions that affect them. By voting five times per year on national issues and at least once per year on state issues, the group takes its results directly to Congress and the state legislators.

The federal NFIB legislative offices are in Washington, D.C., and there are state legislative offices in all fifty state capitals.

SCORE (Service Corps of Retired Executives)

This agency (a subsidiary of the Small Business Administration) gives advice to small-businesspeople. Staffed with retired business owners, executives, and managers, it offers a wealth of valuable counsel on a wide variety of small-business subjects ranging from cost cutting and inventory control to problem solving and business planning. You can arrange for one-on-one counseling, attend prebusiness workshops, or take one of its ongoing training seminars. See your White Pages for local SCORE chapters in your area.

SHRM—Society for Human Resources Management
606 N. Washington St.
Alexandria, VA 22314
(703) 548-3440

This organization counts many thousands of personnel and human resources professionals among its members. It offers a number of training programs, seminars, and written resource materials to interested businesspeople.

Small Business Administration

1441 L St. NW
Washington, DC 20416
(202) 653-6605

For all its faults and foibles, our illustrious federal government does occasionally throw a bone or two to the small business person. This 4,000-person agency has offices in 100 cities and was created specifically to help the small-business professional with advice and expertise, small-business loans, and legal advice on taxes, hiring, health care, insurance, and other issues that keep the small-business owner or operator awake at night. It also creates aid packages to assist new, struggling, or minority-owned small businesses. See your telephone directory for local SBA offices in your area.

Small Business Associations

These are often made up of local like-minded people who can offer you help, support, and even sympathy. Again, check your telephone directory for small-business owners' groups in your local area.

Training Magazine

c/o Lakewood Publications
50 South 9th St.
Minneapolis, MN 55402
(612) 333-0471

One of the bibles for the training and HRD industry, this publication has a staff of skilled writers, many of whom have written business books of note on various subjects related to better people and organizational management.

Bibliography

Albrecht, Karl. *At America's Service*. Homewood, Ill.: Dow Jones-Irwin, 1988.

Albrecht, Karl. *The Northbound Train*. New York: AMACOM, 1994.

Albrecht, Karl. *The Only Thing That Matters*. New York: Harper-Collins, 1992.

Albrecht, Karl. *Service Within*. Homewood, Ill: Business One Irwin, 1990.

Albrecht, Karl, and Steve Albrecht. *Added Value Negotiating*. Homewood, Ill.: Business One Irwin, 1993.

Albrecht, Karl and Lawrence J. Bradford. *The Service Advantage*. Homewood, Ill.: Dow Jones-Irwin, 1990.

Albrecht, Karl and Ron Zemke. *Service America!*, Homewood, Ill.: Dow Jones-Irwin, 1985.

Anderson, Kristin, and Ron Zemke. *Delivering Knock Your Socks Off Service*. New York: AMACOM, 1991.

Carlzon, Jan. *Moments of Truth*. New York: Ballinger, 1987.

Champy, James, and Michael Hammer. *Reengineering the Corporation*. New York: HarperCollins, 1993.

Connellan, Thomas, and Ron Zemke. *Sustaining Knock Your Socks Off Service*. New York: AMACOM, 1993.

Davidow, William H., and Bro Uttal. *Total Customer Service*. New York: Harper & Row, 1989.

John Guaspari. *I Know It When I See It*. New York: AMACOM, 1985.

Peters, Thomas J., and Robert H. Waterman, *In Search of Excellence*. New York: Harper & Row, 1982.

Quinn, Feargal. *Crowning the Customer*. Dublin, Ireland: O'Brien Press, 1990.

Scheuing, Eberhard E., William F. Christopher, et al. *The Service Quality Handbook*. New York: AMACOM, 1993.

Zemke, Ron, and Chip Bell. *Managing Knock Your Socks Off Service*. New York: AMACOM, 1992.

Zemke, Ron, and Chip Bell. *Service Wisdom*. Minneapolis: Lakewood Books, 1989.

Index

STEVE ALBRECHT, B.A., is an experienced author, business seminar leader, and book packager from San Diego, California. He has owned or operated several small businesses, selling products and services since 1987.

He has collaborated on three business books, including *Added Value Negotiating* and *The Creative Corporation* with his father, best-selling author Karl Albrecht, and *Ticking Bombs: Defusing Violence in the Workplace* with Dr. Michael Mantell (all for Irwin Professional Publishing).

He is the managing director for Albrecht Training & Development, a training and consulting firm that offers seminars in added-value negotiating, workplace violence prevention, business writing, and service management.

He is widely known for his written work on law enforcement issues and is the author of *Streetwork, Contact, and Cover* with John Morrison, *One-Strike Stopping Power,* and *The Paralegal's Desk Reference.*

He is also the managing partner of the Oriole Literary Agency in Alpine, Calif.